The Issue of
the Dispensing of
the Processed Trinity
and the Transmitting of
the Transcending Christ

WITNESS LEE

Living Stream Ministry
Anaheim, California

First Edition, 4,000 copies. December 1993.

ISBN 0-87083-741-9

Published by

Living Stream Ministry
1853 W. Ball Road, Anaheim, CA 92804 U.S.A.
P. O. Box 2121, Anaheim, CA 92814 U.S.A.

Printed in the United States of America

CONTENTS

PREFACE

This book is composed of messages given by Brother Witness Lee in Anaheim, California on November 25-28, 1993.

CHAPTER ONE

THE ISSUE OF GOD THE FATHER'S DISPENSING SPEAKING FORTH GOD'S ETERNAL PURPOSE

Scripture Reading: Eph. 1:3-6
Hymns: #501, #841

OUTLINE

I. All the dispensings of the processed Triune God are the spiritual blessings—v. 3:
   A. In the heavenlies.
   B. In Christ.
   C. With which God the Father has blessed the believers, who have been chosen and predestinated by Him.

II. God the Father's dispensing—vv. 4-6:
   A. In choosing the believers—v. 4:
      1. In Christ.
      2. Before the foundation of the world.
      3. To make the believers holy:
         a. That they may be holy as God:
            1) In His life and in His nature after God's kind.
            2) By regenerating the believers, making them His sons.
            3) The unique way to make the believers, common men, holy like God.
            4) Toward the goal of sonship in His predestination to make men His sons that men may become God.
            5) God's salvation is to bring many sons into His glory, to sanctify men, making them

holy like God that they may become God in His nature, life, and expression—Heb. 2:10-11.

b. Without blemish, without mixture, without foreign particles:
   1) The fallen natural human element.
   2) The flesh.
   3) The worldly things.

c. Before Him:
   1) To be holy in the eyes of God according to His divine standard.
   2) To be qualified to remain in and enjoy God's presence.

d. In love:
   1) In the divine love with which God loves us.
   2) In the love which motivates us to love God.

B. In predestinating the believers—v. 5:
   1. Unto sonship.
   2. Through Christ.
   3. To Himself.
   4. According to the good pleasure of His will.

C. To the praise of the glory of His grace—v. 6:
   1. To the praise is the issue of the sonship—Rom. 8:19.
   2. Of the glory—of God expressed.
   3. Of His grace—of the enjoyment of God to express God in His glory.
   4. With which He graced the believers:
      a. Putting them into the position to be the object of God's grace.
      b. That they may enjoy all that God is to them.
   5. In the Beloved:
      a. In His beloved Son, who is His delight.
      b. To make the believers His delight in His enjoyable grace.

Prayer: Lord, we treasure Your blessing; we treasure Your presence; and we treasure Your Spirit, Your blood, and Your word. How we thank You for the divine provision, which is so rich, so prevailing, so refreshing, and so touching. Lord, we look unto You for Your anointing on the whole congregation with every attendant, for Your anointing on every activity, and especially for Your anointing on the speaking and the hearing. Be one with us, Lord. We are here looking unto You. We like to be one with You in Your speaking. Lord, speak Your word in our speaking forth of You. Cover us. We can never forget Your enemy. Defeat him and shame him. Now is the time for the enemy to be shamed, for You to be blessed, and for all of us to be taken care of. Lord, we thank You again. Amen.

The burden of the messages in this book may be expressed in the following four statements:

1. The Father's dispensing in His choosing and predestinating issues in His many sons as His house in sanctification—Eph. 1:3-6.

2. The Son's dispensing in His redeeming and saving issues in the believers as God's inheritance in transformation—Eph. 1:7-12.

3. The Spirit's dispensing in His sealing and pledging issues in God as the believers' inheritance unto their perfection—Eph. 1:13-14.

4. The transcending Christ's transmitting in His rising and ascending issues in His Body as His expression unto the believers' consummation—Eph. 1:19-23.

After I wrote the notes on the book of Ephesians in our Recovery Version of the New Testament, the Lord kept working within me to show me the depths of Ephesians 1. For centuries His people have neglected and even missed the real mark in this chapter of the Bible.

The title of this book is *The Issue of the Dispensing of the Processed Trinity and the Transmitting of the Transcending Christ.* The issue here is the church, the Body of Christ, and this issue is of the dispensing of the processed Trinity and of the transmitting of the transcending Christ. The Trinity has been processed for His dispensing. Also, Christ today is in the highest place in the universe as the transcending One to transmit Himself to the church, His Body. There is a kind of heavenly, spiritual transmission going on all the time from and by the transcending Christ.

The title of this first chapter is "The Issue of God the Father's Dispensing Speaking Forth God's Eternal Purpose." The church as the Body of Christ is the issue of God's threefold dispensing. There are not three kinds of dispensing, but there is one dispensing which is threefold. This dispensing is of the Divine Trinity—the Father, the Son, and the Spirit. The Father's dispensing speaks forth God's eternal purpose.

THE ETERNAL PURPOSE OF GOD

We need to know the eternal purpose of God. Our great God surely has a purpose, and His purpose is the intention of His desire. In eternity past our God had a heart's desire, and this desire became His intention. In this intention there is a purpose. The purpose of God in His intention according to His heart's desire is to have many sons. God desires to have many sons to be His expression in a corporate way.

For this reason He created the universe, and the center of His universal creation is man. For man to live, God prepared the earth, and the earth has to be under the blessing of the heavens. From the heavens the earth receives the sunshine, rain, and fresh air. Then on this earth God created man as the center. Zechariah 12:1 says that God stretched forth the heavens, laid the foundation of the earth, and formed the spirit of man within him. The heavens are for the earth, the earth is for man, and man has a spirit for God so that God can produce many sons.

THE THREEFOLD DISPENSING OF THE DIVINE TRINITY

How could we, the created human beings, become the sons of God? We do not become His sons by adoption but by His begetting. God begot us. In order for a person to beget a child, his life needs to be imparted into that child. This impartation is what we call *dispensing*. We must stress the word *dispensing* when we speak about the intrinsic significance of

Ephesians 1. In Ephesians 1 there is not such a word, but there is such a strong fact.

We need the proper terminology to describe the divine facts in the Bible. In the entire Bible there is not the word *Trinity* or the title *the Triune God,* but there is such a fact in the Bible. This is why the early church fathers came up with these expressions. We have discovered something extraordinary in Ephesians 1. We have seen that the Triune God, for the fulfillment of His intention so that He can be satisfied in His desire, did something wonderful. He dispensed Himself, imparted Himself, into His chosen people, making them all His sons.

John 1 says that Christ gives the believing ones, those who receive Him, the right, the authority, to be the children of God. These children of God are born not of man nor of man's will, but they are born of God directly (vv. 12-13). These children born of God are surely God's sons. This is God's desire, of which God made an intention, and this intention became His purpose, His economy. What the New Testament teaches is this economy (1 Tim. 1:3-4).

God is triune to carry out His economy in His threefold dispensing. He carries out His economy in a threefold way. In Luke 15 the Lord Jesus gives us three parables to show how a sinner gets saved. First, there is the parable of a shepherd seeking for a lost sheep; then there is the parable of a woman seeking for a lost coin; and finally there is the parable of a loving father receiving his returned prodigal son. These parables depict the threefold grace of the Triune God for a sinner to be received back into the Father's house. In the New Testament, there are many portions showing us the threefold doing of our Triune God. In 2 Corinthians 13:14 Paul speaks of the grace of Christ the Son, the love of God the Father, and the fellowship of God the Spirit being with us all. Thus, God's presence is with His believers in a threefold way—in the way of love, in the way of grace, and in the way of fellowship by His Divine Trinity.

Ephesians 1 shows that God has blessed the believers with a threefold dispensing—first by the Father, second by the Son, and third by the Spirit. Eventually, this dispensing will be carried out by the transmitting of the transcending Christ. The Father's dispensing in His choosing and predestinating issues in many sons to form God's household in sanctification. The Son's dispensing in His redeeming and His saving issues in a heritage to God, a treasure to God, as God's private possession. That means all the many sons who issued from the Father's dispensing will become a treasure to God as His heritage. God gains us as His possession, His treasure. Then the Spirit's dispensing in His sealing and pledging issues in God as the believers' inheritance unto their perfection. The issue of God's triune dispensing is the many sons, God's possession, and our inheritance. But there is no church until the transcending Christ comes in to transmit the totality of God's dispensing. The many sons, God's heritage, our inheritance, and the transmitting of the transcending Christ culminate in the church, the Body of Christ.

ALL THE DISPENSINGS OF THE PROCESSED
TRIUNE GOD BEING THE SPIRITUAL BLESSINGS

In Ephesians 1 the dispensing is crucial. Ephesians 1:3 says, "Blessed be the God and Father of our Lord Jesus Christ, who has blessed us with every spiritual blessing in the heavenlies in Christ." The blessings we enjoy are spiritual blessings. No doubt, these blessings are carried out by the Spirit. Otherwise, they would not be called *spiritual blessings*. These spiritual blessings are in the heavenlies and in Christ.

GOD THE FATHER'S DISPENSING
IN CHOOSING THE BELIEVERS TO BE HOLY
BY PREDESTINATING THEM UNTO SONSHIP

The first item of the spiritual blessings is the Father's choosing. We may think that God's choosing is one thing, and God's predestinating is another thing, but this is wrong. We need to look at the grammar of Ephesians 1:4-5. These verses say, "Even as He chose us in Him before the foundation of the world to be holy and without blemish before Him in love, predestinating us unto sonship through Jesus Christ to Himself, according to the good pleasure of His will." These verses do not say He chose us *and* predestinated us. Instead they say that He chose us, predestinating us. *Predestinating* in verse 5 modifies the predicate *chose* in verse 4, so these are not two things. These are one thing. God chose us. How did He choose us? God chose us by predestinating us, by marking us out. To predestinate is to mark out. God chose us to be holy for the sonship. The choosing of God's people for them to be holy is for the purpose of their being made sons of God, participating in the divine sonship.

For a person to have sons, he has to beget them by imparting his life into them. This imparting is dispensing. Without the dispensing of life, no children can be produced. Without God's dispensing, how could God have sons? For God to have sons means that there has been the dispensing of His life. This is fully unveiled in John 1. Christ came to be received. Whoever receives Him, He will give that one the right, the authority, to become a child of God. The right, the authority, to be a child of God is the very divine life dispensed into us. We receive the life of God, and this life is our authority to be the sons of God. We are sons of God because His life has been dispensed into us.

God dispenses Himself in a sanctifying way. God's chosen ones are made His sons by His sanctifying Spirit. God sanctified us to become His sons. He chose us to be holy for sonship. John Wesley said that sinless perfection is holiness, but the Brethren showed that this was wrong. They taught that holiness, sanctification, is not sinless perfection but is a transfer of our position. In Matthew 23 the Lord Jesus said that the gold is made holy, sanctified, by the temple (v. 17) and that the gift is made holy, sanctified, by the altar (v. 19). When the gold was in the market, it was common and worldly. But when the gold was separated unto God through the temple, it was sanctified because its position changed. Likewise, when the gift's location changed from a common place to a holy place, it was sanctified. The teaching of the Brethren concerning positional sanctification is scriptural, but this is not the entire truth concerning sanctification.

Sanctification is to separate God's people unto God for God to work on them and to work in them to make them His sons. God had an intention and made an economy to get many sons. Then the Spirit came to separate the chosen ones unto God so that God could beget them. First, they were sanctified unto God; then through this sanctification they became the object of God's begetting. God came to beget them, making them His sons, and this was through the sanctification of the Spirit. Verse 4 of Ephesians 1 says that God chose us to be holy. Then verse 5 says that He did this by predestinating us unto sonship. Thus, sanctification is unto sonship, for sonship. First, the Spirit comes to sanctify God's chosen people. Then they are ready to be begotten by God into His sonship.

For us to be holy and for us to be sons both require God's dispensing. Without God dispensing His holy nature into our being, how could we be holy? God is the only One who is holy. For us to be holy we need a holy element dispensed into us. When the Holy Spirit comes into us, He brings God's holy nature into us, and that holy nature becomes the holy element with which the Holy Spirit sanctifies us. Stanza 1 of hymn #841 says, "By Thy holy nature / I am sanctified, / By Thy resurrection, / Vict'ry is supplied." His holy nature makes us holy, and His resurrection power makes us victorious. We have God's holy nature imparted into our being, and this holy nature becomes the holy element with which we are made holy. Our being made holy is for us to be sons. The imparting of God's holy nature into us and His begetting us are His dispensing.

SANCTIFICATION FOR SONSHIP IN OUR DAILY LIFE

We may wonder what sanctification has to do with our daily life. This is my burden. We have to realize that sanctification for sonship is still going on. It is not a once-for-all matter. Every day we have to remember that God the Spirit is sanctifying us for God to impart more of His holy nature and holy life into our being to cause us to grow. We all have to grow in the divine life.

Now we need to consider how we can grow. In order for us to grow physically, we need the life within plus the nourishment. A young child has inherited a life from his parents. In other words, his parents have imparted their human life into this child. Then the mother feeds him every day, and he grows with the nourishment in the human life. In principle it is the same in the Christian life. We were born of God. God has imparted Himself into us as life. Now we need to grow by being nourished in the life of God. Our birth is a beginning, not a graduation. After our birth, we need to grow in the life of Christ, in the divine life, in the eternal life, with the proper nourishment in the Spirit.

Both sanctification and the sonship are always carried out by the Spirit. This is why Ephesians 1:3 calls this a spiritual blessing, a blessing by the Spirit. Today we must learn to live by the Spirit, to act according to the Spirit, to have our being altogether by the Spirit, with the Spirit, and according to the Spirit (Rom. 8:4). As long as we have our being by the Spirit and act according to the Spirit, we are ready to grow in the divine life. Then we need some nourishment. We can be nourished in these three ways: by reading the holy Word, by listening to the spiritual speaking, and by coming to the meetings. This nourishment causes us to grow.

I am concerned that many dear ones among us are seeking after the Lord, but they still are not on the way of the growth in life. If we are driving a car for a long distance, we need to find the freeway and get on it. Once we get on the freeway, we have to be careful about the direction we take. If we get on the right freeway with the right direction, then our driving is okay. We need to get on the way of the growth in the divine life in the right direction. We still need some revelation to see the right way to grow in the divine life according to the New Testament teaching.

In order to grow, we must deal with the Spirit. We must get ourselves right with the Spirit. We must have our entire being in the Spirit, and walk, behave, and act according to the Spirit all day long. When the parents are with their children, they have to behave themselves according to the Spirit in order to be kept in the divine life. Many times the parents are too free and unrestricted in what they say to their children. They may be afraid of making mistakes when they talk to others, but they do not have any care when they speak to their children. This is wrong. We should not say anything according to our taste. Instead, we have to be regulated, corrected, and adjusted by saying everything and doing everything according to the Spirit.

It is the Spirit who sanctifies us unto sonship. It is the Spirit who begets us that we may be born of God (John 3:6). God chose us to be sanctified unto sonship. To be sanctified unto sonship is altogether a matter by the Spirit, in the Spirit, and with the Spirit. I am concerned when I see a number of dear saints who have been in the recovery for many years with no growth. Although they may meet, read the Bible, and listen to the messages, they do not care for the Spirit. Instead of taking care of the Spirit when they speak, they freely gossip and criticize others. Although they say that they love the Lord, love the recovery, and love the church life, they do not care a bit for the Spirit. This is wrong. We have to take care of the Spirit. Today this Spirit, who is wrapped up with sanctification and with God's sonship, is in our spirit (Rom. 8:16; 1 Cor. 6:17). If we desire to take care of the Spirit, we should first take care of our spirit.

The Bible says that we should not provoke our children to anger (Eph. 6:4). When we are angry with our children, we often provoke them. In dealing with our children, we have to take care of our spirit. We need to check, "Does our spirit agree with us, or are we acting according to our emotion?" We should deny our emotion and turn to our spirit. Then in our spirit, the Spirit will speak to us. When we are becoming angry with our children, the Spirit may say, "Go into your room and pray. Don't talk to your children at this time." That is a kind of sanctification. When we pray, the speaking Spirit will continue to speak. He may lead us to read a portion of the Word. Then we are nourished, and we grow in the divine life with the spiritual nourishment. If we do not care for our spirit in our family life, we surely cannot have a pleasant household, and God cannot sanctify us for His sonship and His household.

We need to take care of our spirit in everything. When a brother buys a necktie, he should not buy it according to his taste. If he buys it according to his taste, this is wrong. Even in buying a tie, he should take care of his spirit. What would our spirit say to us when we go shopping? If we would listen to our spirit, the Holy Spirit will speak more in us.

Today we are promoting the prophesying of all the saints. We want to see the saints speak for the Lord. Some saints, however, have determined not to speak in the meetings. They come to the church meetings, but they sit at the back in silence. The leading ones who are taking care of the saints may be afraid to say anything to these ones about speaking, because they are afraid they will stop coming to the meetings. Thus, they may come to the meetings for years without speaking anything for the Lord. They have been regenerated, and they love the Lord, love the recovery, and love the church, but they just would not speak. Be assured that if this is your case, you will not grow at all in the Lord.

You must take care of your spirit. Get down on your knees in your bedroom to pray, and see what your spirit would say to you. Your spirit will tell you that you are stubborn and that you should go along with the church to speak for the Lord. If you take care of your spirit, the divine Spirit will take the opportunity to speak many more things to you. Then you will come to the meeting by taking care of your spirit. You may even confess to the saints, "Dear saints, I regret that I have not spoken for the Lord in the meetings." The whole church will be happy. Then as you continue to speak, the Holy Spirit will speak to you so that you have even more to speak. Then you will see that the speed of your growth in life will fly like an airplane. Within half a year, you will grow much in Christ and be much more sanctified unto much more sonship. By your growth in life, you will become not just a son but an heir of God to inherit the riches of God (Rom. 8:17). Then you will be so useful in the church life. You will become a supplier to supply, to minister, the bountiful supply of the Spirit to all the congregation.

Dear saints, this is my burden. We should not think that Ephesians 1:4 and 5 transpired once for all. Sanctification for sonship is still going on. Day by day, however, we do not live in our sonship, because we do not care for the sanctifying Spirit speaking and working in our spirit. We must turn to our spirit, realizing that we have been sanctified and regenerated by the Spirit. This sanctifying and regenerating Spirit has much to say to us. He still wants to sanctify us more and more that we may participate in the sonship more and more. Then we will grow, and the Father will have a pleasant household. If we care for our spirit and let the Spirit speak to us, we will grow as sons to become heirs, grown-up persons, to inherit all the riches of God. Then we can be a part of His pleasant household. The blessings in Ephesians 1 start from God's choosing for us to be sanctified that we might be more and more in the sonship of God. This should be a daily matter.

CONCLUDING NOTES TO CHAPTER ONE

1. Without dispensing His holy element into our being, how could God make us holy? Especially for God's sonship, there is the need for God to dispense His life and nature into our being.

2. The Father's dispensing in His choosing and predestinating of the believers issues in His sonship through His sanctifying of His chosen people, making them holy as He is in His life and in His nature, to make them like God in the divine life and nature, but without His unique Godhead. This is the divine sanctification unto (for) the divine sonship. This is the center of the divine economy and the central thought of the revelation in the New Testament. Such a divine sanctification is carried out by the sanctifying Spirit (Rom. 15:16). The divine sonship is accomplished by the regenerating Spirit, who is the Spirit of the Son of God (Gal. 4:6).

I hope that these concluding notes will be a reminder to us that sanctification is still going on for our development in the sonship of God that we may grow. We will have a stronger and richer church life as we continue to take care of the divine sanctification for the sonship by the Spirit.

CHAPTER TWO

THE ISSUE OF GOD THE SON'S DISPENSING SPEAKING FORTH THE ACCOMPLISHMENT OF GOD'S ETERNAL PURPOSE

Scripture Reading: Eph. 1:7-12
Hymns: #972, #750

OUTLINE

I. Through His redemption—v. 7:
  A. The forgiveness of offenses.
  B. Through His blood.
  C. According to the riches of His grace.
II. To make the believers the inheritance of God—vv. 8-11:
  A. By His abounding grace—vv. 8-10:
    1. In all wisdom and prudence—v. 8:
      a. Wisdom is for God to make a plan and purpose a will in eternity.
      b. Prudence is for God to apply what He has planned and purposed in time.
    2. To make known to all the mystery of His will—v. 9:
      a. According to His good pleasure.
      b. Which He purposed in Himself.
    3. Unto the economy of the fullness of the times—v. 10a:
      a. *Economy* refers to God's plan for dispensing Himself into His chosen people.
      b. *Fullness* refers to the completion of all the times for God's dispensing.
      c. *Times* refers to the ages:
        1) The age of sin.

        2) The age of the law.

        3) The age of grace.

        4) The age of the kingdom.

   4. To head up all things in Christ—v. 10b:

     a. The issue of God's dispensing in all the ages.

     b. Especially through the divine dispensing to the church so that the church is saved from the universal collapse in death and darkness and grows in life to be headed up in Christ in peace and harmony.

B. In God's designation, making the believers a chosen inheritance of God—v. 11:

   1. According to the purpose of God, who works all things according to the counsel of His will.

   2. Transforming, in the great salvation of Christ, the believers into a treasure (an inheritance of worth) to God in the life element of Christ, to whom they have been redeemed.

   3. That they may inherit God as their inheritance.

III. To the praise of God's glory—v. 12:

A. In the believers who have first hoped in Christ.

B. By the angels and all the positive things in the universe.

C. Mainly in the millennium and ultimately in the new heaven and new earth.

In Ephesians 1 the most striking thing is the dispensing plus the transmitting. The dispensing is done by the processed Trinity, and the transmitting is done by the transcending Christ. What the Trinity dispenses is for producing the many sons of God, the heritage to God as His treasure, His private possession, and a glorified body as the consummation of the Trinity's dispensing. This is revealed in verses 3 through 14. In these verses there are the many sons of God, God's heritage, and our glorified body, but the church is not yet mentioned. We need to realize that these items are all for the church, the Body. The dispensing of the processed Trinity produces the constituents for the church, but there is still the need for the formation of the church. The formation of the church does not depend upon the Trinity's dispensing but upon the transcending Christ's transmission with His surpassing, transcending power which raised Him up from the dead, seated Him at the throne of God, subjected all things under His feet, and made Him the Head over all things to the church (vv. 19-23).

I was told many years ago that the book of Ephesians is on the church. When I was with the Brethren, they told me that Adam and Eve were a type of Christ and the church. Later, I met Brother Watchman Nee and became one of his close co-workers. He told us strongly that the church comes out of Christ just as Eve came out of Adam. That was a great help to me. It is wonderful to see that the church has come out of Christ. But still at that time in my studying of the holy Word, I had not entered into the intrinsic significance of this matter. For years I was wondering how the church comes out of Christ and how Christ produces the church with His life. Eventually, I came out of mainland China and stayed in Taiwan from 1949 to 1961. During that period of time, the Lord opened my eyes. I saw that the coming out of the church is altogether a matter by the Holy Spirit and in our spirit. Without these two spirits—the Holy Spirit and our spirit—there is no possibility to have the coming out of the church. There is no possibility for the church to come into existence.

THE DIVINE SANCTIFICATION FOR SONSHIP

We also have seen something further concerning the truth of sanctification. This has been a great subject among us in the recovery for the past seventy years. We studied and investigated this, spending much time to get into others' writings. But we were not fully satisfied with what we had seen. It was not until this year, 1993, that I saw the full intrinsic significance of sanctification. I saw this when the church in Anaheim was spending time to review our life-study on Hebrews, which was given in 1975. That life-study was very thorough, yet I did not see fully at that time how the sanctification of the Spirit is related to the sonship. Hebrews 2:10 says that the Lord as the Captain of God's salvation will lead many sons into glory. Then verse 11 speaks of the One who sanctifies and those who are being sanctified. When I considered these two verses, my eyes were opened to see that sanctification is for sonship. This is new light.

When I saw this, I entered into a fuller understanding of Ephesians 1:4-5. Verse 4 says "to be holy," and verse 5 says "unto sonship." We need to put these two phrases together—"to be holy unto sonship." This shows us again that sanctification is for sonship. The Greek preposition for the word *unto* is very profound. It means "resulting in." To be holy results in the sonship. God's sonship comes to us through the Holy Spirit's sanctification. The concluding notes of chapter one of this book point out that the divine sanctification is unto the divine sonship. I hope that the Lord will have mercy on all of us to pick up this thought. Divine sanctification is not for sinless perfection nor is it merely for a change of our position. It is for the sonship and results in the sonship. We call it the divine sanctification because it is a matter of the Spirit Himself. It is a matter of the Triune God.

Now I would like to present a full view of the divine sanctification as unveiled in the holy Word. God has a desire. Based upon His desire, He made an intention with a purpose. This is His eternal economy, *oikonomia* (Gk.). This economy was made by the Father, accomplished by the Son, and carried out and applied to us by the Spirit. The carrying out of the eternal economy of God is by the Spirit's sanctification. The Spirit's sanctification is the carrying out of God's eternal purpose in four steps.

Seeking Sanctification

The first step of the divine sanctification by the Spirit is His seeking sanctification. This is the Spirit's coming to seek out God's chosen people who became lost. The seeking sanctification is fully unveiled in the second parable in Luke 15. There the Spirit is likened to a woman seeking a lost coin by lighting a lamp and sweeping the house (v. 8). She sought this lost coin finely. Eventually, she found it. Actually, the lost coin was the prodigal son. Due to the Spirit's seeking and finding, the prodigal son woke up. He came to himself (v. 17). He made the decision to rise up and go back to his father to repent.

John 16 goes on to show that this seeking Spirit is also the convicting Spirit. He convicts all the lost sinners of sin in Adam, of righteousness in Christ, and of the judgment for Satan (vv. 8-11). Man's full repentance is the result of the work of the seeking and convicting Spirit.

First Peter 1:2 tells us that this seeking and convicting of the Spirit is the sanctification of the Spirit before the sprinkling of the blood upon the repentant sinners. This shows that the seeking sanctification was before our repentance and believing in Christ. Actually, our repentance and believing were due to the seeking Spirit, the convicting Spirit. We were lost in sin and among a heap of sinners, but the seeking Spirit came to seek us out. As a result we woke up, repented, returned to God, and asked Him to forgive us. This was the result of our Father's choosing with His predestinating in eternity past along with His Spirit's coming in time to seek us out and convict us. This seeking, this convicting, is the seeking sanctification.

Regenerating Sanctification

At the juncture we repented and believed in the Lord Jesus, the same Spirit, the seeking Spirit, sanctified us further by regenerating us. We were born of the Spirit (John 3:5) and

God as the Spirit came into our spirit (Rom. 8:16; 2 Tim. 4:22). Now we are the sons of God, the children of God. The seeking Spirit woke us up and brought us back to the Father. We repented and believed in the Lord Jesus. We received Christ, and the Spirit sanctified us further, making us the children of God. This is the second step of the divine sanctification, the regenerating sanctification.

The Father put Christ's redeeming blood upon us, just like the loving father put the best robe upon the returned prodigal son (Luke 15:22; Heb. 13:12). Also, the sanctifying Spirit entered into our spirit with God's life to make us children of God. Now we have the blood of Christ without and the life of God within. All our offenses have been forgiven through the blood, the redemption of Christ, and our spirit has been regenerated. The Spirit's regenerating sanctification transpired in our spirit (John 3:6).

Transforming Sanctification

After regeneration, the next step of the Spirit's sanctification is His transforming sanctification. This takes place in our soul. Our regenerated spirit has never been a problem to us. Our problems always come from two sources: our soul (comprising our mind, emotion, and will) and our body. Our untransformed mind, emotion, and will give us much trouble. Following the regeneration of the sanctifying Spirit in our spirit, the sanctifying Spirit carries out His continuous sanctification to transform us in our soul. We were regenerated, sanctified unto God, in our spirit, but we need the sanctifying Spirit's further work to sanctify our soul. This is the transforming sanctification.

This transformation implies renewing and conformation to the image of Christ. While the sanctifying Spirit works to sanctify us, we are being transformed. Second Corinthians 3:18 tells us clearly that transformation is by the Lord Spirit. This is a strong proof that the Spirit's transformation is His work to keep sanctifying us. Romans 12:2 says that we are to be transformed by the renewing of our mind. The transformation of the sanctifying Spirit first renews our troublesome mind. For us to be transformed, we need some new element added into us to carry away our old element and replace us with the new element. This is a kind of metabolism which results in a metabolic change within us. Thus, we become another person in our thinking, in our feelings, and in our intentions. The Bible says we are being transformed from the old man into the new man. This is a further step of the sanctifying Spirit, the transforming sanctification. Now we have the seeking sanctification, the regenerating sanctification, and the transforming sanctification, which includes the renewing and the conforming to the image of Christ.

Glorifying Sanctification

Our full transformation will one day consummate in our glorification. That will be the work of the sanctifying Spirit to glorify us in our body. Another thing that bothers us besides our soul is our poor, vile body. Lust, weakness, sickness, and death are present in our corrupted body. Our body is really vile, but one day we will be glorified and transfigured in our body (Phil. 3:21). Our spirit has been regenerated, our soul is being transformed, and our body will be transfigured, changed into a glorious body with no more lust, weakness, sickness, or death. This is the glorifying sanctification.

When all these four steps of the divine sanctification (seeking sanctification, regenerating sanctification, transforming sanctification, and glorifying sanctification) take place, we will be glorified. We will be qualified to meet the Lord. By that time we will be able to shout, "We have been fully sanctified!" Today we are like a butterfly who is still in the cocoon. Eventually, we will come out of the cocoon. We will not walk on this earth; we will fly. This is the consummating sanctification.

Now we have seen the proper teaching of the New Testament concerning sanctification. Sanctification is the hinge of God's carrying out of His eternal economy. The sanctifying Spirit in God's sanctification first sought us out and then regenerated us, making us sons of God. If a cat begets kittens, those kittens are baby cats. In the same way, God begot us to make us the sons of God. To make us the sons of God is to make us "baby gods," having God's life and nature but not His Godhead. In life, in nature, and in expression we are the same as He is, because we are born of Him. Thus, we are not only the children of God, we are not only the sons of God, we are not only the heirs of God, but we are also the "baby gods." The kittens, the baby cats, are surely cats because they are according to the cats' kind. God created everything according to its kind. Man, however, was created according to God's kind because he was created in God's image (Gen. 1:26). Later, we men were born of God, not only bearing God's image but also having God's life and nature. Thus, we become God in life and in nature, but not in the Godhead. This is what the sonship means.

Now we can see the intrinsic significance of Ephesians 1:4-5. God chose us to be holy, predestinating us unto sonship. God dispensed Himself into His chosen people so that His chosen people could be holy as He is. Our being made holy results in our being made sons of God, making us God in life and in nature, but not in the Godhead. The carrying out of God's eternal economy is hinged on the divine sanctification unto (for) sonship.

THE ISSUE OF THE SON'S DISPENSING

Now that we have seen the issue of the Father's dispensing, we want to go on to see the issue of the Son's dispensing, which speaks forth the accomplishment of God's eternal purpose. This is revealed to us in Ephesians 1:7-12. These verses say, "In whom we have redemption through His blood, the forgiveness of offenses, according to the riches of His grace, which He caused to abound to us in all wisdom and prudence, making known to us the mystery of His will according to His good pleasure, which He purposed in Himself, unto the economy of the fullness of the times, to head up all things in Christ, the things in the heavens and the things on the earth, in Him; in whom also we were designated as an inheritance, having been predestinated according to the purpose of the One who works all things according to the counsel of His will, that we would be to the praise of His glory who have first hoped in Christ."

Through God's abounding grace, Christ accomplished

redemption for us, and this redemption is for the forgiveness of our offenses. This is somewhat easy to understand. But the above verses are full of difficult expressions and words such as *mystery, will, good pleasure, purposed, the economy of the fullness of the times,* and *to head up all things in Christ.* We need to see the intrinsic revelation and significance of this difficult portion of Ephesians 1.

God, according to His desire with an intention, made an economy, and the center of the divine economy is God's desire to have many sons. God created the universe for His many sons, but man became fallen. Now in this universe there are two ugly things: the rebellion of Satan with his angels and the fall of man. These two things brought the entire universe into a collapse. The universe was created by God in a very beautiful order. But due to Satan's rebellion and man's fall, this beautiful order was turned upside down. After man's fall, in man's second generation Cain murdered his younger brother Abel (Gen. 4:8). All the evil things, such as murder, fornication, stealing, cheating, and lying, show that today's world is in an upside-down situation. Everything is upside down today. This upside-down situation has even invaded the church. Some who rebelled even tried to bring the upside-down situation of the human race into the recovery.

But God would never give up His eternal economy. He is very consistent and insistent. He first applied His anticipated salvation to mankind, so that mankind could continue on this earth. Then eventually, He Himself came to be a man. He did not only create man, but He also came to be a part of mankind, to be one with man. He lived a human life for thirty-three and a half years. Then He was qualified to go to the cross to die a marvelous death, an all-inclusive death. In that death He solved the problem of sin, the problem of the old man, the problem of the world, the problem of Satan, and even the problem of death. He solved every problem, and He ended and cleared up everything of the old creation. He rested for three days, and then He rose up.

In His resurrection, He became another kind of person. In incarnation as God He became man (John 1:14). Now in resurrection as man He became a life-giving Spirit (1 Cor.

15:45b). God became a man to solve all the problems, to terminate all the negative things in the whole earth and even in the whole universe. Then as the last Adam, the last man, the end of mankind, He rose up to become a life-giving Spirit. God who is joined with man became a life-giving Spirit in His divinity and in His humanity.

A number of people oppose this scriptural revelation. They think that the three of the Godhead are separate and that we cannot say the Son became the Spirit. They just care for their theology. They do not care for the spiritual, divine fact. The Bible says in 1 Corinthians 15:45b, "The last Adam became a life-giving Spirit." The Lord in whom we believe, Jesus Christ, who is the last Adam, has become a life-giving Spirit. Paul said that Christ lives in us (Gal. 2:20a). If Christ were not the life-giving Spirit, how could He live in us? Christ lives in us, works in us, and even makes His home in our heart (Eph. 3:17). Second Timothy 4:22 says, "The Lord be with your spirit." If He were not the Spirit, how could He be with us in our spirit? At the most He could only be among us, not within our spirit.

When I came to this country, a number of saints told me that they never knew that they had a human spirit. Many Christians today do not believe that Christ as the last Adam became a life-giving Spirit, nor do they believe that they have a spirit. They do not have these two key points. Without these two key points, there is no way to live the Christian life. The Bible tells us that God created a spirit within man (Gen. 2:7; Prov. 20:27; Job 32:8; Zech. 12:1). The Bible also tells us how God became a man and died to accomplish redemption to end the old creation. Then He rose up. In His rising up He became another person—the life-giving Spirit—to enter into us. In the morning He rose up. In the evening He came back to the disciples to breathe upon them, saying, "Receive the Holy Spirit" (John 20:22). By that time He was the life-giving Spirit to be received by His disciples. From this point onward, the key points of the Christian life are the life-giving Spirit and our spirit.

Today He is the life-giving Spirit. He not only rose up but also transcended to the heavens and passed through the heavens (Heb. 4:14). The ascended Christ has at least twelve statuses. Each status qualifies Him to minister in a certain realm. In His ascension He was enthroned as Lord of all and appointed, assigned, to be the Christ of God (Acts 2:36). He is the Leader of all the rulers (Acts 5:31a). He is the Savior (Acts 5:31b). Even though we may want to save people, we cannot do it. But He can do everything. Because He is the omnipotent One, He can save us. He is the High Priest (Heb. 4:15; 7:26) and the Advocate (1 John 2:1b). He is the Intercessor, interceding for us (Heb. 7:25). He is also the Mediator of the new covenant (8:6) and the surety of the new testament (7:22). He is the Life-giver (John 10:10b), the Comforter (14:16-17), and the Lamb-God (Rev. 22:1b). He is in the heavens ministering all the time. The key point is that today He is the life-giving Spirit. Without being the life-giving Spirit, He could never be the High Priest ministering to us. He could never be the Life-giver. He could never be the Comforter. He is the life-giving Spirit to execute His covenant, to carry out what He has accomplished through His all-inclusive death.

Ephesians 1 says that in Him we have redemption. He redeemed us back to Himself. We were fallen in Adam. That was our location. But Christ's redemption redeemed us out of that location and brought us into Himself as the realm and the element. Actually this realm and this element are the Spirit. He is the life-giving Spirit, and He has redeemed us out of Adam into Himself as the life-giving Spirit. As the redeemed ones of Christ, we all should declare, "I am in the Spirit!" We are not on the earth, nor are we merely in the heavens; we are in the Spirit. The Spirit is our location. The Spirit is our realm. The Spirit is our element. In this realm and with this element, Christ is working every day to transform us.

The Spirit, who is the realm and the element, is the sanctifying and transforming Spirit. He is transforming us metabolically, making us a particular treasure to become God's private possession, even God's heritage, God's inheritance (Eph. 1:11). God wants to inherit something. He wants to inherit those who were once sinners and who have become a treasure. Today we are in the cocoon, but eventually we will become a butterfly. We are expecting to be glorified, and God is also expecting to see that we are glorified. Then He will have a complete treasure. This may seem like a dream, but one day this dream will be fulfilled.

The transforming Spirit makes us right-side up. Before we were saved, we were in an upside-down situation. We were collapsed in death and darkness. But the Spirit in His seeking sanctification brought us back to God. We believed into Christ, and the Spirit continued to sanctify us by regenerating us. Then this Spirit, who is Christ Himself, continues His sanctifying work to transform us every day, making us right-side up.

A brother may talk to his wife apart from the Spirit in an upside-down way. But gradually the Lord transforms this brother to make him realize that his way is not the Lord's way. The Lord's way is not in our flesh or in our American way of thinking. His way is in our spirit. Eventually, the Lord will work in this brother again and again to turn him to his spirit. There the Holy Spirit meets him to shine over him, enlighten him, and speak to him in a personal way. The Spirit may say, "From now on don't talk to your wife without My speaking." This will make this brother right-side up.

Bit by bit the transforming Spirit is making us upright. We are not merely corrected or adjusted outwardly but transformed inwardly. The very Christ who is living in us, working in us, and making His home in us is transforming us day by day. When a person moves into a new house, he makes many adjustments. Christ is making His home in us and making many adjustments within us.

In our marriage life, we are upside down much of the time. The wife's attitude toward her husband may not be proper. It is upside down. But every day the indwelling Christ is fixing His dwelling place. He is transforming us, making us right-side up. This transformation makes us a treasure. God is making us His treasure by transforming us.

As we are being transformed, we are being made right-side up, that is, we are being headed up under Christ. It is a beauty to see this. In the Lord's recovery, we should be Jesus lovers who have been headed up under Christ. When we are headed up, there is no turmoil, no fighting, no debating, no confusion, and no collapse. Instead, everything is in a good order. We Jesus lovers should take the lead to be headed up in Christ. Then eventually Christ will have all things in heaven and on earth headed up under Him. God has given Him to be the Head over all things, but all things today would not be headed up. But we, His lovers, should take the lead to be headed up in Christ. Today's whole universe is in an upside-down situation. The whole universe needs to be made right-side up, to be headed up. We are the Jesus lovers, who are willing in Christ's redemption to be transformed by the sanctifying Spirit to be made right-side up. This is why the Lord needs a recovery. Among us there should be no struggling, no fighting, and no debates. There should just be fellowship and submission.

This is all due to the dispensing of the Son. The Son's dispensing in His redemption and His transformation through the sanctifying Spirit issues in the heritage prepared as a treasure to God. The Father's dispensing results in a group of sons. The Son's dispensing results in all of us being made a treasure. Now God not only has a group of sons, but also has all the sons becoming His treasure, His heritage. Many of us came to this conference from a long distance because we want to be right-side up. What is the Lord doing today in His dispensing? He is making us right-side up by transforming us in our soul. This transformation includes our being renewed and conformed to the image of Christ, resulting in a heritage produced for God.

THE SON'S DISPENSING TO MAKE THE BELIEVERS GOD'S INHERITANCE UNTO THE ECONOMY OF THE FULLNESS OF THE TIMES TO HEAD UP ALL THINGS IN CHRIST

We all have seen that the first main point in Ephesians 1 is the threefold dispensing of the processed Divine Trinity. The Father's dispensing is to make us holy unto sonship. God chose us with a purpose to make us different from everything in this universe, that is, to sanctify us and to make us holy for the purpose that we could be begotten of God to be His sons. The secondfold aspect of the dispensing is somewhat complicated. For the firstfold dispensing there are only two verses, but for the secondfold dispensing of the Son, there are verses 7 through 12.

Verses 10 and 11 are some of the hardest verses in the whole Bible for readers to apprehend. These verses say, "Unto the economy of the fullness of the times, to head up all things in Christ, the things in the heavens and the things on the earth, in Him; in whom also we were designated as an inheritance, having been predestinated according to the purpose of the One who works all things according to the counsel of His will." God's economy will be consummated at the fullness of the times. In God's economy there are four main ages, and these ages are called "the times." There are the age of sin from Adam to Moses; the age of law from Moses to Christ's first coming; the age of grace from Christ's first coming to His second coming; and the age of the kingdom. In these four ages, God is working to recover His lost creation back to His purpose. Then at the fullness of the times, God's economy will be consummated. This economy is to head up all things in Christ, the things in the heavens and the things on the earth.

Verse 11 says that we have been designated as an inheritance. *Designated* in Greek means "chosen or assigned by lot." We have been designated, marked out, and assigned by lot to be God's inheritance as a treasure. In the secondfold dispensing of the Trinity, Christ has redeemed us. In His redemption He has redeemed us back to Himself, even into Himself, and He has imparted Himself into us. Thus, the redeeming Christ has become a realm in which we are enjoying the dispensing. He is also the element by and with which we are being renewed and transformed to be a treasure, a heritage of worth, to God.

God created us, but we fell into sin, forsaking God as our Head. Then we became a collapse. Since Satan's rebellion plus man's fall, the entire universe has lost its order. It became collapsed in death and darkness. Now Christ came to redeem us out of Adam into Christ, and this redemption implies the forgiveness of our sins. After forgiving us, Christ brought us back to God, to Himself. Now we are in Christ as a realm and an element. In this realm and with this element, after we have been redeemed, the Triune God is now in Christ as the life-giving Spirit dispensing His element into us daily and hourly to renew us day by day and transform us hour after hour, making us a treasure, an inheritance of worth.

We were in the collapse as God's enemies, but Christ redeemed us out from Adam, from sin, and from the collapse. Then in this redemption, gradually, as we are growing in Christ, we are headed up in Christ. This heading up is the order of the church, the order of Christ's Body. In our physical body there is an order. Things are not upside down but right-side up. Generally speaking, the church is a setting up of the proper divine order. This will lead to a consummation at the fullness of the four ages when all things in the heavens and on the earth will be headed up in Christ. That will be the New Jerusalem in the new heaven and the new earth depicted in Revelation 21 and 22. The New Jerusalem will be the consummation of today's church.

In Christ's redemption the life-giving Spirit is dispensing hourly into us the element of the processed and redeeming Triune God in Christ to renew us and transform us. While we are being transformed, we are being regulated and put into an order. That order is the church. This heading up leads to the final heading up at the fullness of the ages. That will be the new heaven and new earth with the consummation of the church as the New Jerusalem, in which everything will be in order under one Head. The whole universe will be new at that time. Being new means to be out of the collapse. There is no more collapse in the New Jerusalem in the new heaven and new earth. Today the church life should be a miniature of that situation.

The firstfold dispensing of the Divine Trinity is to produce sons, but we need the secondfold dispensing to redeem us back to God in Christ. In this realm with this divine element we are being renewed, transformed, and brought into order. There is the heading up today in the church which leads to the final and consummate heading up at the fullness of the times, the ages, in the new heaven and new earth. There we can see the New Jerusalem with everything in order. This is the issue of the secondfold dispensing of the Son, which speaks forth the accomplishment of God's eternal purpose.

CONCLUDING NOTES TO CHAPTER TWO

The Son's dispensing in His redemption and transformation of the believers issues in a heritage of worth, a private possession, transforming God's chosen people, with Christ as the element of life, into a treasure to be God's inheritance as His personal possession. This is to bring the redeemed universe from the collapse into a good order, to head up all things (collapsed in death and corruption) under Christ through the church built up as the Body of Christ. This is also carried out by the Lord as the transforming Spirit (2 Cor. 3:17-18), to make God's chosen people a new creation by the renewing of the transforming Spirit.

CHAPTER THREE

THE ISSUE OF GOD THE SPIRIT'S DISPENSING SPEAKING FORTH THE APPLICATION OF GOD'S ACCOMPLISHED PURPOSE

Scripture Reading: Eph. 1:13-14
Hymns: #539, #493

OUTLINE

I. In sealing the believers—v. 13:
   A. As the compound, anointing, life-giving, and indwelling Spirit promised by God.
   B. Through the believers' hearing of the word of the truth, the gospel of their salvation—v. 13a.
   C. Through the believers' believing in Christ.
   D. To saturate the believers continuously unto the redemption of their body—Eph. 4:30.
   E. For transforming the believers into a treasure to God as His inheritance—Eph. 1:11; 2 Cor. 3:18:
      1. By His renewing—Titus 3:5; Rom. 12:2b.
      2. With the life element of the all-inclusive Christ—Phil. 1:19b.
   F. To make the believers a mark of God's image—2 Cor. 3:18b:
      1. With the substance of God.
      2. For the expression of God.
II. In pledging to the believers—v. 14a:
   A. Through the sealing.
   B. As a foretaste of God.
   C. For a guarantee of God as our inheritance.
   D. Unto the redemption of the body of the believers as God's acquired possession.

III. To the praise of God's glory—v. 14b:
  A. In the expression of God's image.
  B. In the enjoyment of God's riches.
IV. The dispensing of the Divine Trinity issuing in the Body of Christ as the organic constitution (Eph. 4:4-6) with:
  A. God the Father as the source.
  B. God the Son as the element.
  C. God the Spirit as the essence.

THE TWO STAGES OF CHRIST'S MINISTRY

The Bible shows us that there are two stages in the ministry of our Lord Jesus Christ. To understand the New Testament we must realize and comprehend these two stages of the Lord's ministry.

Christ's Earthly Ministry, from His Incarnation to His Crucifixion

The first stage was Christ's earthly ministry, from His incarnation to His crucifixion, that is, from His birth to His death. In this first stage He ministered as a man, speaking forth God in His flesh (John 8:26; 12:49-50). First, He lived for thirty years to become fully mature. According to Numbers 4:23, thirty years is the full age for a servant of God. At the age of thirty He came out to minister for three and a half years, traveling back and forth between Galilee and Judea. In the Gospel of Matthew He spoke much concerning the kingdom, and in the Gospel of John He spoke much concerning the divine life, which is the eternal life. Then He went to the cross and He died an all-inclusive death to solve all the problems in the universe between God and His creation. After finishing His work in His death, He rested, keeping the Sabbath.

In His Resurrection Christ Being Born as the Firstborn Son of God and Becoming the Life-giving Spirit

Then, from that rest He rose up in His resurrection. In His resurrection He was born. All Christians realize that Christ was born once. He was born in Bethlehem, of Mary, to be a man. But the New Testament shows us that the Lord Jesus was born a second time. Incarnation was His first birth, a birth in which He as God became a man. Resurrection also was a birth to Jesus Christ as the last Adam. To this last Adam, this last man, resurrection was another birth. In this birth He was born to be the firstborn Son of God. This is clearly revealed in Acts 13:33, which tells us that Christ was born in His resurrection to be the firstborn Son of God.

Before His resurrection Christ was already the only begotten Son of God (John 1:18; 3:16, 18). From eternity to eternity He is God's Only Begotten. However, in His incarnation He became a man; He put on humanity. As the only begotten Son of God, He was divine, but in His first birth He picked up humanity and put it upon Himself. Thus, from that day forward He was no longer merely God; He was also a man. He was the complete God and the perfect man. He was such a wonderful person. Nevertheless, there was a problem: As a divine person He had a human part that was not divine and that had nothing to do with God's Son. That human part was the Son of Man, not the Son of God. When He finished His earthly ministry, at the time when He accomplished God's eternal redemption, He finished His work. Hence, He rested. At the end of His crucifixion He declared from the cross, "It is finished!" (John 19:30) because His earthly ministry, that is, the ministry for the accomplishment of redemption, was finished, consummated, completed. Therefore, He slept and He rested.

However, God's economy was not yet finished. That was just the first part of God's economy; it was not the greatest part. The greatest part of God's economy was yet to come. Therefore, after He rested for three days, He rose up. On the one hand, the New Testament says that God raised Him up; on the other hand, it also says that He Himself rose up (Acts 2:24 and note 24[1]; 10:40-41). Both God and He brought Him out of death, Hades, and the tomb. In 1 Corinthians 15, a chapter that deals particularly with the matter of resurrection, verse 45 says, "The last Adam became a life-giving Spirit." According to this verse, in His resurrection, as a man, the last man, the concluding man, the last Adam, Christ became a life-giving Spirit. He was also born to be the firstborn Son of God. This means that in His resurrection, Christ "sonized" His humanity. He made His humanity also a part of the Son of God. Now Jesus Christ as the Son of God has two natures, the divine and the human. After His resurrection He came back to His disciples as the Spirit (John 20:19-29). At that time He asked His disciple Thomas, "Bring your finger here and see My hands, and bring your hand and put it into My side" (v. 27). This means that the resurrected Christ still had His physical body. We cannot understand how the Lord can be both physical and spiritual at the same time. Nevertheless, in His resurrection Christ was born to be the firstborn Son of God as the life-giving Spirit.

Christ's being the firstborn Son of God indicates that many sons of God will follow. His birth in resurrection and through resurrection was not just the delivery of one son; it was the delivery of the firstborn Son and of many sons as well. According to 1 Peter 1:3, we all were regenerated, that is, reborn, with Christ in His resurrection. In His resurrection He was delivered as the firstborn Son of God, and we were delivered as the many sons of God. We all were included in that great delivery (Eph. 2:6a), in which millions of sons of God were born.

We all need to realize that the birth of the firstborn Son with the birth of the many sons created another world. In this universe there is another world, a spiritual, heavenly, and divine world. The unbelievers know only this present human world. They do not know anything about the other world. But we have been regenerated out of the human world and into another world that is spiritual, heavenly, and divine. Thus, Philippians 3:20 tells us that we are heavenly citizens, and Ephesians 2:6 says that we have been seated together with Christ in the heavenlies.

Christ's Heavenly Ministry
in the Heavens and in Our Spirit

Many Christians say that Christ's ministry was finished at the end of His death. However, the Bible says that Christ's ministry still continues after His death. His earthly ministry was accomplished and recorded in the four Gospels in the New Testament. After the Gospels and the Acts, the apostle Paul wrote fourteen Epistles, from Romans through Hebrews. In these fourteen Epistles Paul opened the heavens, showed us that we are seated in the heavens, and unveiled to us that today Christ in the heavens as the resurrected One and the newborn One, the firstborn Son of God, is very busy. He is busy in His heavenly ministry. He accomplished redemption in

His earthly ministry, but He applies this redemption to us in His heavenly ministry.

Today Christ is both in the heavens and in our spirit (Rom. 8:34, 10; 2 Tim. 4:22). We may use electricity to illustrate how Christ can be in two places at the same time. The same electricity is simultaneously in the power plant and in our homes. This is not two electricities but one electricity in one transmission. It is the transmission that connects our homes with the power plant. Today Christ is the same as electricity. As the life-giving Spirit, He is there in the heavens and also here in our spirit. In this way He has brought us all into the heavens. Today the heavens are in our spirit. Hebrews 10:19 and 22 tell us to come forward to the Holy of Holies and to enter the Holy of Holies, and 4:16 tells us to come forward with boldness to the throne of grace. After reading such verses, we may wonder where the Holy of Holies and the throne of grace are today. If they were only in the heavens, how could we come forward to them, and how could we enter the Holy of Holies? Today, the Holy of Holies is not only in the heavens; it is also in our spirit. This is why Hebrews 4:12 stresses our spirit to the uttermost. This verse says, "For the word of God is living and operative and sharper than any two-edged sword, and piercing even to the dividing of soul and spirit and of joints and marrow, and able to discern the thoughts and intentions of the heart." According to this verse, we must have the capacity to discern our spirit from our soul. The problem today is that many Christians do not have the capacity to discern their spirit from their soul. Many even say that the spirit and the soul are the same.

Today in the Lord's recovery we have a clear sky and a clear vision to see that Christ is in the heavens, and He has brought the heavens into our spirit. This corresponds to the ladder that Jacob saw in his dream at Bethel (Gen. 28:12). That ladder stretched from the earth to the heavens, and the angels of God were ascending and descending on it. It brought the earth to the heavens and joined the heavens with the earth, making the heavens and the earth one. In John 1:51 the Lord Jesus told His disciples that they would "see heaven opened and the angels of God ascending and descending on the Son of Man." Christ today is the ladder in His resurrection. Because of this, when we speak the Lord's word in His ministry today, we speak not only on the earth but also in the heavens. We speak in our spirit, where the heaven is on the earth. We have much to speak because we are speaking in the heavens, yet we are still on earth.

Many Christians today know only Christ's earthly life and ministry. Their knowledge is limited to what is recorded in the four Gospels. They do not like to go further. A number of years ago one group of Christians declared that they followed only Jesus and they would not follow Paul. They accepted only the teaching in the four Gospels; they would not accept Paul's fourteen Epistles. Today, in name, all Christians accept the twenty-seven books of the New Testament, yet, in actuality, many know only the things of Christ in the four Gospels. They know very little concerning Christ in the fourteen Epistles of Paul.

If Christ's ministry were only on the earth in the flesh, He could not dispense anything into us. In the earthly ministry of Christ there is only the accomplishing; there is no dispensing. Whatever Christ accomplished was objective to us, not subjective, until He became a life-giving Spirit. In His resurrection He began to impart, that is, to dispense, His divine life into us. The dispensing in Christ's ministry did not begin from the earth. At the time when Christ went out of death and entered into resurrection, He imparted His divine life into all of us to regenerate us (1 Pet. 1:3). At that time His dispensing began.

Today Christ is in the heavens, and He is very busy. In Galatians 2:20 Paul said, "It is no longer I who live, but it is Christ who lives in me." For Christ to live in us means that He is not idle in us but is very active. As the Spirit He not only lives in us, but He also dwells in us (Rom. 8:11). Furthermore, He is now making His home in us (Eph. 3:17). He also strengthens us, sustains us, supports us, comforts us, supplies us, takes care of our case in the heavenly court, and intercedes for us. In His heavenly ministry He does everything for us. As He ministers in His heavenly ministry, He has many statuses: He is the Lord of all (Acts 2:36a), the

Christ of God (Acts 2:36b), the Leader of all the rulers and the Ruler of the kings of the earth (Acts 5:31a; Rev. 1:5b), the Savior (Acts 5:31b), the High Priest (Heb. 4:15; 7:26), the Advocate (1 John 2:1b), the Intercessor (Heb. 7:25), the Mediator of the new covenant (8:6), the surety of the new testament (7:22), the Life-giver (John 10:10b), the Comforter (14:16-17), and the Lamb-God (Rev. 22:1b). As such a One, He sustains us and supports us with the bountiful supply of the Spirit of Jesus Christ (Phil. 1:19).

I have been speaking for the Lord for more than sixty years. Today I still have many subjects to speak on, and I also have the strength to minister. As far as I am concerned, I am nothing. Nevertheless, the more I speak, the more I have to speak. Although I have spoken on Ephesians a number of times, I still have something further to speak because I am sustained, supported, strengthened, and supplied by Christ with the bountiful supply of the Spirit of Jesus Christ. The One who supplies me is not just the Spirit of God; today the Spirit of God has become the Spirit of Jesus Christ.

First Corinthians 6:17 says, "But he who is joined to the Lord is one spirit." This also is the good news of the gospel. Do you realize you are one spirit with the Lord? We are one with God. As those who are one spirit with God, we are not small persons. We are one with God; we are a part of God (John 15:5a; Eph. 5:30). Athanasius, a young theologian who participated in the Council of Nicaea, said concerning Christ, "He became man that we might be made God" and "The Word was made flesh...that we, partaking of His Spirit, might be deified." According to Athanasius' word, God became a man that man might become God in life and in nature (but not in the Godhead). We are not only God in life and in nature, but we are one with God.

The Spirit today is not merely the creating God. This Spirit is the God who became incarnated, crucified, and resurrected, and who also became a life-giving Spirit. This is the reason that we can be one spirit with Him. He has become a life-giving Spirit, and we have a spirit created by Him (Zech. 12:1) and regenerated by Him (John 3:6). In this universe these two wonderful spirits, the life-giving Spirit and the human spirit regenerated and indwelt by the Spirit, have come together to be mingled as one. This is surely the good news.

We need some new songs to sing about our being one with God in the spirit. We all need to praise the Lord, saying, "Praise You, Lord Jesus! Today You are the Spirit. You were God and You became a man, and now in Your resurrection You have become the life-giving Spirit." In this life-giving Spirit He can and He did dispense whatever He has, whatever He is, whatever He accomplished, whatever He is doing, and all His attainments and obtainments into our being. Christ is the embodiment of the Triune God (Col. 2:9). Thus, the Father's dispensing actually is a part of His dispensing. The Spirit's dispensing also is a part of His dispensing.

THE SPIRIT'S DISPENSING
IN HIS SEALING THE BELIEVERS

The dispensing of the Spirit is carried out in His sealing the believers (Eph. 1:13). If we want to seal something, we must have a seal which bears a certain image, and we must also have the sealing ink. The seal with the sealing ink can be applied to a piece of paper to seal the paper. The sealing makes the sealing ink and the paper one. The sealing ink soaks the paper, saturates the paper, anoints the paper, is mingled with the paper as one, and is even constituted together with the paper to be one constitution. We have been sealed not with ink but with the sealing Spirit, who is the saturating Spirit, the anointing Spirit, the soaking Spirit, and the sanctifying Spirit. The more He saturates us, the more He sanctifies us. We are like pieces of paper. When a piece of paper is sealed, the sealing action does not stop. The sealing still goes on to saturate the paper with the sealing ink, to soak the paper with the sealing ink, to make the paper absolutely one in constitution with the sealing ink. Eventually, the sealed paper becomes full of ink.

The Spirit by whom we are sealed, soaked, and saturated is the Lord Himself (2 Cor. 3:17). He is the Spirit, and the Spirit is the seal. This seal as the Lord Himself seals us, saturates us, and soaks us. This too is the good news of the gospel.

When a husband is about to exchange words with his wife, he should wait so that he can remain under the sealing for a while. This will cause him to forget the exchanging of words. Instead, he will be full of praises. He will rejoice because he has been soaked and saturated as a result of being under the sealing of the Lord as the life-giving Spirit. The sealing of the Spirit within us regulates us, controls us, and causes us to behave ourselves properly. Often after a church meeting or a ministry meeting we all are happy, singing, praising, and full of joy because we have been under the Spirit's sealing.

To Saturate the Believers Continuously unto the Redemption of Their Body

According to Ephesians 1:13-14 the Spirit's sealing will continue unceasingly unto the redemption of our body (4:30). The Greek preposition *unto* does not mean "until"; it means "resulting in." The Spirit is sealing us, resulting in the redemption of our body. We need to believe that this sealing of the Spirit is still going on. As this sealing proceeds, we even have the sense that our lust, our sickness, our weakness, and our deadness are being reduced. After these things are fully reduced, we will be redeemed in our body. Our body will be transfigured and glorified. This is the consummation of the Spirit's sanctification.

As we have seen, the sanctification of the Spirit began with the Spirit's seeking us out, and it continues through His regenerating, His transforming, which includes His renewing and conforming, and then His sealing. Sealing implies transformation, and it also implies renewing and conformation. The Spirit's sealing is transforming us, renewing us, and conforming us to the image of Christ (Rom. 8:29). This will result in the transfiguration of our body, which will be our glorification. At that time the sanctification of the Spirit will be consummated, reaching its peak.

Day by day we are under the sealing of the Spirit. This sealing is our daily salvation. The more we are soaked, saturated, and sealed by the Spirit, the more we are saved.

If we do not experience such a daily salvation, we may lose our temper and become angry and argue with others. However, now the sealing is going on to save us from our temper, from our anger, and from our evil speaking and evil thinking concerning the other saints. Every day, every hour, morning and evening, this saving is going on. It is this saving that can save us to the uttermost, as mentioned in Hebrews 7:25. Through the sealing there is a continuous saving as we remain under the sealing. Ultimately, this sealing will result in the transfiguration of our bodies to bring us all into glory. At this juncture we will be fully sanctified, from our spirit, through our soul, and to our body. At that time our spirit, soul, and body will be wholly sanctified (1 Thes. 5:23).

This is the heavenly ministry of the resurrected and transcending Christ. In His transcending He is ministering the entire sanctification of the Spirit to us. On the one hand, it is the Spirit who performs the sanctification in us. On the other hand, it is Christ who ministers the sanctification to us. Christ, the heavenly One, is ministering to us a sealing, a saturating, and a soaking that saves us from our unpleasant feelings concerning our fellow believers. As we are under such a heavenly ministry, we feel quite pleasant toward the saints. We are saved by the sealing in Christ's heavenly ministry. In this way we are sanctified, we are matured, and we have the growth in life.

Today, our Christ is not ministering on the earth. He is not ministering in Galilee and Judea. He is ministering in us, in our spirit. He is ministering in all our spirits simultaneously. While He was on the earth, at the time He ministered in Galilee, He could not minister in Judea. But today He can minister in thousands of us at the same time. I can testify that every day He ministers the heavenly ministry to me to meet my need. As a little servant of the Lord, I am caring for the churches and the saints in seventeen regions on this earth. This causes me to have a great need. Although I am limited, I have One who is never limited. He is the Lord, the Christ, the Leader, the Savior, the High Priest, the Advocate, the Intercessor, the Mediator, the surety, the Life-giver, the Comforter, and the Lamb-God. He is so much! Therefore, in all my labors I am happy and pleasant. We do have an unlimited, heavenly Christ ministering to us in the heavens and in our spirit. Through the rich supply of His heavenly ministry, our work becomes our rest and our enjoyment. Every day I work under a sealing that goes on continuously, day and night.

For Transforming the Believers into a Treasure to God as His Inheritance

Eventually, this sealing is for God's heritage. This sealing transforms the believers into a treasure to God as His inheritance. In the Father's dispensing we were all made sons of God, but in the dispensing of Christ, the Son, we, the many sons of God, have been made a treasure as God's heritage, as God's inheritance. The Greek verb translated "were designated" in Ephesians 1:11 means "to choose or assign by lot." Hence, the clause "were designated as an inheritance" literally means that in Christ we were designated as a chosen inheritance for God. This inheritance was chosen through the transformation of the sealing Spirit. Thus, in the Son's dispensing all the sons of God become a treasure to God.

To Make the Believers a Mark of God's Image

In the Spirit's dispensing He seals us, putting a mark upon us. This mark bears an image with a form. The more we are sealed, the more we bear the image of God (2 Cor. 3:18b; Col. 3:10). The more we are sealed, the more we look like God. Eventually, the image we bear becomes not just an image, not just a mark, but an expression. Through the Spirit's sealing we express God.

THE SPIRIT'S DISPENSING IN HIS PLEDGING TO THE BELIEVERS

Eventually, this sealing becomes a pledging (Eph. 1:14). The more a piece of paper is sealed, the more the sealing ink will be on the paper. Likewise, the more the Spirit seals us, the more the Spirit shares with us God's element. This sealing element becomes a pledge to guarantee that God is our inheritance. The sealing declares that we are God's inheritance. Eventually, such a sealing becomes a pledge guaranteeing that God is our inheritance. The Spirit's pledging guarantees that God is our inheritance. How good it is that we are God's inheritance and He is our inheritance! Although a brother may lose his job, he is still God's inheritance, and God is still his inheritance. Under the Spirit's sealing and pledging, we do not need to worry about anything. No matter what may happen to us, we are still God's inheritance, and He is still our inheritance. This is because we are participating in the Spirit's sealing and pledging as His dispensing.

The Spirit's sealing and pledging eventually make us God in His life and nature, but not in His Godhead. They also cause us to have the full assurance that we are God's and God is ours.

CONCLUDING NOTES TO CHAPTER THREE

1. The Spirit's dispensing in His sealing and pledging issues in the redemption of our body, the transfiguration of our vile body into a glorious body like that of Christ.

2. The Spirit's sealing of the believers as God's heritage is the Spirit's anointing, saturating, and soaking of the believers with the divine element of Christ's riches of life in the believers. This is for the Spirit's transforming of the believers metabolically.

3. The first section of the divine revelation presented to us in the book of Ephesians is the Triune God's triune dispensing. The three aspects of the Triune God's triune dispensing are the three sections of the Holy Spirit's sanctification performed in the believers. The first section is the regenerating sanctification in our spirit to bring forth many sons for God to form an organism for God's corporate expression, which is the organic Body of Christ, the church. The second section is the transforming sanctification in our soul to transform the regenerated believers by renewing them and conforming them to the glorious image of Christ that they may become a heritage of worth, a treasure to God as God's private possession. This will bring the upside-down

universe into an upright order by heading up all the collapsed things under Christ. The third section is the consummating sanctification in our body to transfigure the believers' body by redeeming their vile body into God's glory that they may be fully and wholly sanctified in their spirit, soul, and body to be a consummated corporation of God's many sons who are matured in the processed Triune God as their life that they may express God as the New Jerusalem for eternity.

4. Hence, the carrying out of God's eternal economy is the Spirit's sanctification. The accomplishment of God's eternal economy hinges on the sanctification of the Spirit. Thus, the Spirit's sanctification has very much to do with the Body of Christ, which is the issue of the Spirit's sanctifying work. It is because of this that Ephesians 4:4 says "one Body and one Spirit," and the sanctified life of the saints is the infilling of the sanctifying Spirit in our spirit (Eph. 5:18). Our new man is created according to God in His holiness by the renewing in the spirit of our mind.

5. Since the book of Ephesians is the revelation of the church as the issue of the Spirit's triune dispensing, it stresses the Spirit's infilling for the saints' holy living and the divine holy element for the saints' holy constitution. We, the pursuers of Christ, must pay our full attention to our inward constitution with the divine element and to our outward living by the Spirit's inner filling.

CHAPTER FOUR

THE ISSUE OF THE TRANSMITTING OF THE TRANSCENDING CHRIST

Scripture Reading: Eph. 1:15-23

Hymns: #885, #890

OUTLINE

I. The apostle's prayer for the believers—vv. 15-20a:
   A. Thanking God for their faith in the Lord Jesus and their love to all the saints—vv. 15-16a.
   B. Asking God, the Father of glory—vv. 16b-20a:
      1. To give the believers a spirit of wisdom and revelation in the full knowledge of Christ—v. 17.
      2. To enlighten the eyes of their heart that they may know—v. 18a:
         a. What is the hope of God's calling—v. 18b.
         b. What are the riches of the glory of His inheritance in the saints—v. 18c.
         c. What is the surpassing greatness of God's power toward the believers, according to the operation of the might of God's strength, which God caused to operate in Christ—vv. 19-20a.

II. Christ's transcending—vv. 20b-22b:
   A. Raised from the dead—v. 20b.
   B. Seated at God's right hand in the heavenlies—v. 20c:
      1. Far above all rule, authority, power, and lordship—v. 21a.
      2. Above every name that is named not only in

this age but also in that which is to come—v. 21b.
- C. Having all things subjected under His feet—v. 22a.
- D. Given to be Head over all things—v. 22b.
III. Christ's transmitting—vv. 22c-23:
- A. To the church, His Body—v. 23.
- B. Transmitting:
  1. His accomplishments in His incarnation, crucifixion, and resurrection.
  2. His victory in His resurrection.
  3. His attainments and obtainments in His ascension.
- C. Consummating in His heavenly ministry of:
  1. The Lord of all—Acts 2:36a.
  2. The Christ of God—Acts 2:36b.
  3. The Leader of all the rulers—Acts 5:31a.
  4. The Savior—Acts 5:31b.
  5. The High Priest—Heb. 4:15; 7:26.
  6. The Advocate—1 John 2:1b.
  7. The Intercessor—Heb. 7:25.
  8. The Mediator of the new covenant—Heb. 8:6.
  9. The surety of the new testament—Heb. 7:22.
  10. The Life-giver—John 10:10b.
  11. The Comforter—John 14:16-17.
  12. The Lamb-God—Rev. 22:1b.

THE THREEFOLD DISPENSING
OF THE PROCESSED TRINITY

I am so grateful to the Lord that we can touch the intrinsic revelation of Ephesians 1. This revelation is altogether wrapped up in God's threefold dispensing—the Father's dispensing, the Son's dispensing, and the Spirit's dispensing. These are not three kinds of dispensings. This is just one dispensing which is threefold. Firstly, the Father chose us, predestinating us to be His sons in holiness (vv. 4-5). This implies the Father's dispensing. If the Father had not dispensed Himself as the holy nature into us, how could we be holy? In the whole universe there is only One who is holy—God Himself. Furthermore, if the Father had not dispensed Himself into us, how could we become His sons? We are His sons not by adoption but by birth. Birth implies dispensing. Our Father begot us. In that begetting He spontaneously dispensed His life into us. So in the Father's dispensing we all were made His sons in sanctification.

Also, as lost ones we needed redemption, so the Son came to redeem us out of Adam (vv. 7-12). Adam was the sphere and the element into which we fell. But Christ came in the flesh as a man, went to the cross, and died an all-inclusive death to rescue us from Adam and bring us into Christ Himself as another realm. Now we are in Christ. In the New Testament, this is a strong phrase—*in Christ*. To be in Christ is a great thing. We have been redeemed into a sphere, into a realm, and also into an element. This element is living, organic, and working. Christ is the life into which we have been redeemed.

Now Christ as the life-giving element is working within us. Any kind of life works and operates. When the divine life works, this is the working of the life-giving Spirit. Christ as the last Adam became a life-giving Spirit (1 Cor. 15:45b). This means that the Spirit works with Christ as life to transform us. In this transformation, we are being made right-side up. We were in Adam, altogether upside down in a situation of collapse. In the whole universe, there is nothing but collapse, and we were a part of that collapse. But Christ redeemed us out of the collapse into Himself as life. Now this life element is working within us to adjust us, to bring us back to the divine order.

Now we all are in His Body being headed up under Him. In the past we did not have any head. Rather, we made ourselves the head. Consider today's society. Everyone is their own head. In today's modern families, the children even become heads. Today's universe, today's world, today's America, and today's society are a collapse. But we have been redeemed out of this collapse into Christ, our realm, our element, and our Head. He is now working within us all the time by transforming us.

We are now in Christ to be transformed all the time. As we remain in Christ, we experience the sealing of the Spirit. The Spirit today is not just the Spirit of God. He is the Spirit of Jesus Christ (Phil. 1:19), the life-giving Spirit, and this life-giving Spirit is Christ Himself. Such a life-giving Spirit is the consummation of the Triune God. The entire Triune God has been consummated in this Spirit. In this Spirit there are the Father, the Son, the Spirit, Christ's divinity, His humanity, His incarnation, His human living, His crucifixion, His resurrection, and His ascension. All these are compounded in this consummation of the Triune God, which is the life-giving Spirit, and such a Spirit came to seal us.

Sealing is a matter of saturation, a matter of soaking. The sealing ink has a spreading effect. I like this phrase *spreading effect*. Eventually, the entire piece of paper is saturated with the sealing ink. Such a spreading effect is a finer dispensing. When we were saved, we were sealed and this sealing will continue until our body is redeemed (Eph. 4:30). This sealing came upon us to spread finely within us in everything—in the way we think, in the way we talk, in the way we deal with people, in the way we cut our hair, etc. We need to realize that even the way we cut our hair impresses people with who we are. We should bear the Lord's testimony and expression in everything we do and in everything related to our person.

When I came to this country in the sixties, I observed the hippies with their long hair, beards, and wild clothing. A number of young people who came into the recovery in the sixties were like this. While I was ministering the word, some of them sat on the front row in their bare feet. But thank the Lord, they all got saved. After a short time, their clothing began to change, their long hair and beards were cut off, and they began to wear shoes. Who adjusted them? I did not say a word to them. They changed from being hippies to gentlemen because of the sealing of the Spirit. The sealing Spirit moves within us to soak us and saturate us, transforming us metabolically.

This sealing is unto a result, and this result is the redemption of our vile body, the transfiguration of our vile body, which is our glorification. In the first fourteen verses of Ephesians 1 we see the threefold dispensing, from the Father's choosing to our being brought into glory. This is the completion of God's dispensing. God brings us fallen sinners from the heap of collapse into Christ to be sealed under the gradual, fine dispensing day by day for the full course of our Christian life. Eventually, as we remain under this dispensing, we will be matured and made ready to be transfigured in our body. Then we will be in glory.

Such a dispensing issues in a spiritual, divine constitution. This constitution is the church as the Body of Christ. The church is not an organization. It is an organism, and this organism is a constitution. It is constituted with the Triune God mingling Himself with His chosen people in humanity. In Ephesians 4:4-6 there is a record or a portrait of this constitution. Verse 4 says, "One Body and one Spirit." The one Body is the structure, the frame, and within this frame there is the one Spirit, who is the essence. The one Lord is the element (v. 5), and the one Father is the source (v. 6). The Spirit as the essence, the Lord as the element, and the Father as the source are constituted into this frame of humanity. A group of chosen human beings becomes the very structure, the very frame, of this constitution, and they are constituted with the Triune God as the essence, element, and source. In the universe there is such a wonderful constitution, and this constitution is the church as the organism of the Triune God for Him to move, to act, to fulfill His purpose, and to express Himself.

We human beings created by God became fallen, so God came to redeem us to carry out His choosing and accomplish His purpose. Then He dispensed Himself as everything into our being to create a spiritual, heavenly, divine constitution, that is, the Body of Christ as the church. This is wonderful, yet there is something more.

FOUR LAYERS OF OPPOSITION
WHICH CHRIST OVERCAME
IN HIS TRANSCENDING

We need to realize that in the universe there are four layers of opposition, four layers of trouble. The first layer is Hades with death. This is the bottom layer of trouble. Hades with death retains people. Hades even sends out death to gather and grasp people. When death comes, no one can resist it. So death captures people and brings them into Hades. Hades becomes a prison and the gates of Hades retain people. No one can open these gates, and no one can overcome them. Within these gates there are many dead persons, and no one can come out of them. But the Lord Jesus said, "I will build My church, and the gates of Hades shall not prevail against it" (Matt. 16:18). In the universe there is a struggle going on between the gates of Hades and the dead ones. Lazarus and the rich man are there (Luke 16:19-31). The rich man was struggling to get out of Hades, but the gates would not release him. This is the first layer of the problem in the universe.

The second layer is the human world. Ephesians 1 says that when Christ ascended to the heavens, He transcended above all the human names, names at His time and names in the ages to come (Eph. 1:21). History tells us that since Christ's time, many big names have risen up against Him and against the church. Caesar Nero was the strongest one. Napoleon was one, and Hitler became one. But Christ ascended far above every name that is named. First, He rose up from the dead. Many dead persons were struggling to get out of the gates of Hades. They could not do it, but Christ could. He rose up, the gates of Hades opened for Him, and He came out of Hades. He resurrected from the dead to overcome Hades. Then in His ascension, He transcended above all the names, not only the big names opposing Christ and His church but also the small names. We were there among the small names opposing Him. He transcended above us. This is another layer of trouble which Christ overcame. In Russia, Lenin began a kind of revolution against God and against the church. Eventually, after just seventy years, who defeated whom? Christ defeated Lenin. Jesus transcended above all the names. No one can oppose Jesus on this earth without being defeated.

The third layer of trouble is in the air. In the air is the power of darkness—the rulers, the authorities, the power, and the lordship in the air (Eph. 1:21). In the air among the angelic race there are rulers, authorities, power, and lordship, good ones and bad ones. Even on the earth among human beings there are also the rulers, authorities, power, and lordship (see Eph. 1:21 and note 21[1]).

We also need to see that the fourth layer of trouble is in the third heaven. Even the third heaven was polluted by Satan's presence. The book of Job tells us that Satan appeared in the third heaven before God at a heavenly council, accusing God's people (1:6-12a; 2:1-6). Thus, even the third heaven needs to be under the feet of Christ. Hebrews 4:14 tells us that Christ passed through the heavens, and 7:26 tells us that He has become higher than the heavens. He is not only higher than Hades, than the earth, and than the air but also higher than the heavens. Therefore, Christ actually passed through four layers: Hades, the earth, the air, and even the third heaven. Christ had to transcend through Hades, through the earth, through the air, and even through the third heaven to reach a place that is far above even the third heaven. Hebrews 7 tells us that today Christ is higher than the heavens. He is there as the highest One to transmit not only His authority but also His transcending power to the church that the church may be formed.

We should not think that the universe is so simple. We are speaking of things which are not visible to the eyes of worldly people, but they are visible to us. This is why Paul, before sharing this portion of the Word, prayed, asking the

Father to give His people a spirit of wisdom and revelation that they may have the full knowledge of Him (Eph. 1:17). What Paul spoke in Ephesians 1 cannot be understood by the people of this world. Even I am greatly concerned that among the Christians, very few are clear in their spirit. Many do not even admit that they have a spirit. How poor this is. But Paul prayed, "Father, give Your chosen people a spirit of wisdom to understand and of revelation to see." We need a spirit of wisdom to understand all these mysterious things and a spirit of revelation to see them.

Formerly, we may have been veiled concerning God's eternal purpose. Now the veil has been taken away and a revelation has been presented to us. We can see that in this universe there are four layers of trouble. The bottom layer is Hades, the second layer is the earth with all the troubling persons, and the third layer is the air with Satan's power of darkness and all his rebellious angels. The good angels are also there, and the Bible tells us that they sometimes fight with the bad angels (Dan. 10:13, 20). The highest layer is the third heaven, which was polluted by Satan's presence.

Christ transcended far above all the layers of trouble. America spent billions of dollars to build something to land on the moon. But compared to where Christ landed in His ascension, landing at the moon is like taking one step on a very high stairway. Paul prayed that we would see the surpassing greatness of God's power which operated in Christ to raise Him from the dead out of Hades and to seat Him on high at God's right hand in the heavenlies (vv. 19-20). Christ died; He was there in Hades. But after three days He came out of Hades. Then He transcended through the heavens, and He is sitting on the throne of God. By doing this He is above all the rulers, authorities, power, and lordship, good ones and bad ones among the human race and also among the angelic race. He is above all names in this age and in the coming age. These names include yours and mine. I was opposing Christ for some time, but one day I was subdued by Him. Many of us are ex-opposers of Christ.

We all were subdued by Him because He transcended above all of us in His transcending power.

This power subjected all the things under His feet (v. 22a) and gave Him a gift for Him to be the Head over all things (v. 22b). Now Christ is sitting on the throne. He has come out of Hades, and He is above all the things on the earth and in the air, and He is higher than the heavens with all things subjected under His feet. He is the Head over all things. What a picture! Who can resist this Head of all things who has become the very Head of the church? Who can oppose this One? And who can oppose His Body, the built-up church? This is why He said in Matthew 16, "I will build My church." Christ is building the church in His heavenly ministry as He is sitting on the throne with all things subjected under His feet as the Head over all things. The gates of Hades cannot prevail against such a built-up church. History tells us that the Caesars, including Nero, rose up against Christ and the church. Later, Hitler and Mussolini were opposing Christ, but they were defeated. Who is prevailing today? The transcending Christ and the Body of this Christ are prevailing today.

I was raised up by the Lord as a little servant to Him. But from the first day that I rose up to speak for Him in His recovery, opposition came. Before that day people warmly welcomed me to speak to them. But a number of my inviting friends became my opposers when I took the Lord's way in His recovery. The denominations rose up against me in my city. I have also experienced opposition from the political circle. When the Japanese invaded China, I was arrested and put into their prison twice. The second time I was in prison for thirty days. At that time it was nothing for the invading army of Japan to kill a Chinese person, but the Lord preserved me. Later, I came to this country, and I put out messages on Christ as the Spirit and on our human spirit. Then some evil books were published to oppose these truths. The opposition is always there to try to blockade us, but Christ has transcended. The Lord's recovery is still going on, and the Lord will not stop until He has accomplished His purpose according to His heart's desire.

THE TRANSMITTING OF THE TRANSCENDING CHRIST TO BRING FORTH THE BODY OF CHRIST AND THE FINE DISPENSING TO CONSTITUTE THE BODY OF CHRIST

Now we need to see the transmitting of the transcending Christ. The power plant does not dispense a little electricity in a gentle and fine way. It transmits the electricity strongly. If more power is needed, the amperage can be turned up. This is not dispensing but transmitting. The ascended Christ, the transcending Christ, not only dispenses but also transmits. Seemingly He is hiding Himself. But actually Christ is very active. The power plant does not need propaganda to tell people that it is acting. The power plant is very quiet, but the transmission is going on.

The church is now spreading over the whole earth because of the transmission of the transcending Christ. He is transmitting His great power to us. This is the power that raised Him up from the dead and that caused Him to transcend above all human beings and above all the angelic race, including all their leaders, rulers, authorities, power, and lordship. This is the power that seated Him at the height of the universe, the power that subdued and subjected all things under His feet, and the great power that gave Him to be the Head over all things. In the transmission of this power, He builds up the church.

On the day of Pentecost, that was not a dispensing. That was a transmission. The coming of the Lord's recovery to this country and our being caught for the Lord's recovery were due to the transmission of the transcending Christ. The divine dispensing is to constitute the Body of Christ, and the divine transmission is to form the Body of Christ. Day by day, we enjoy the fine, gradual, mild, gentle dispensing in the Lord's dealings with us. The Lord in His dispensing tells a brother not to talk to his wife in a certain way. In His dispensing He tells a sister not to spend twenty-five minutes to comb her hair in a certain way, when she says she does not have even five minutes to pray. Through His dispensing He impresses a brother not to wear a certain tie that is too loud. A pursuer of Christ should be so proper in what he wears to bear a proper testimony. This fine dispensing in the Lord's dealings with us constitutes the Body of Christ, whereas His transmitting brings forth the Body of Christ.

On the day of Pentecost, a rushing wind came (Acts 2:2). That was the transmission to form the Body of Christ. But that Body formed by the transmission of the transcending Christ needs much dispensing. After the church was formed in Acts 2, problems came in. In Acts 5 there was a couple deceiving God the Spirit (vv. 1-11). In Acts 6 there was murmuring among the saints (v. 1). The divine dispensing was needed to clear up all of these things. The church is here, but it may not be so peaceful. Transmission transpired, but dispensing still needs to continue, to go on.

I am speaking something which I have learned. I learned these things mostly from listening to Brother Watchman Nee. He helped me a lot. I worked directly with him for eighteen years. Before those eighteen years, I corresponded with him for seven years. Thus, my relationship with him was for twenty-five years. He was only two years older than I. What could keep us for such a long time without one bit of dissenting? Just before Brother Nee died in prison, he told his prison roommate who was saved through him, "When you get out, find a brother by the name of Witness Lee, and let him know that I never gave up my faith....When you see him, you see me. And his word is my word." What kept Brother Nee and me in such a oneness? The continuous dispensing. We experienced the transmission of the transcending Christ, but day after day for many years we were kept in one accord by the finer dispensing of the sealing Spirit. The consummation of the Triune God as the life-giving Spirit is all the time sealing us with His fine dispensing to transform us. We are here in one accord by His gracious dispensing of grace.

I hope we can see that the church was formed and came into being by His transmission. This is the transmission of the transcending One's great power that raised Him from among the dead in Hades and that caused Him to transcend to the Father's throne above all the human race and the angelic race. This is the great power that subdued and subjected all things under His feet and that gave Him to be

Head over all things to the church. This great power is toward us who believe (Eph. 1:19) and to the church (v. 22). This indicates that the divine power is transmitted into us to cause the church to come into existence. After the church comes into existence, daily, hourly, and moment by moment, by His mercy and grace, we must learn the lesson to be supplied with His gradual, slow, and fine dispensing in a threefold way by the Father, the Son, and the Spirit. This is the revelation in Ephesians 1.

Christ's transmitting is to the church, His Body. The surpassing greatness of God's power which operated in Christ is toward us. God subjected all things under His feet and gave Him to be the Head over all things to the church. This shows the divine transmission. He is transmitting all His accomplishments in His incarnation, crucifixion, and resurrection into us. He also transmits His victory in His resurrection. Finally, He transmits all His attainments and obtainments in His ascension.

This consummates in His heavenly ministry. He is in His heavenly ministry in the following twelve statuses:

1. The Lord of all (Acts 2:36a).
2. The Christ of God (Acts 2:36b).
3. The Leader of all the rulers (Acts 5:31a).
4. The Savior (Acts 5:31b).
5. The High Priest (Heb. 4:15; 7:26).
6. The Advocate (1 John 2:1b).
7. The Intercessor (Heb. 7:25).
8. The Mediator of the new covenant (Heb. 8:6).
9. The surety of the new testament (Heb. 7:22).
10. The Life-giver (John 10:10b).
11. The Comforter (John 14:16-17).
12. The Lamb-God (Rev. 22:1b).

Because He is such a Lord, such a Christ, and such a Ruler that can manage all the things on this earth, He can be the all-inclusive, all-capable, omnipotent Savior to save us. As the Advocate, He is the One who takes care of our case in the heavenly court. He is ministering in the heavens in the above twelve statuses. This is why Philippians 1:19 speaks of the bountiful supply of the Spirit of Jesus Christ! This is the supply from Him in these twelve statuses in His heavenly ministry. What a bountiful source of supply!

THE THREEFOLD DISPENSING OF THE DIVINE TRINITY TO PRODUCE THE MATERIALS AND THE UNIQUE TRANSMISSION OF THE TRANSCENDING CHRIST TO FORM THESE MATERIALS INTO THE CHURCH

Ephesians 1 is on the church as the issue of two matters. The first matter is the threefold dispensing of the Divine Trinity. This matter is deep and fine, but it is not very hard for us to get into it. The second matter is the onefold unique transmission of the transcending Christ. This matter is very difficult to see. This is why after the mentioning of the first matter, Paul did not go on directly to the second matter. Instead, he prayed. He realized that we are short of the capacity to understand and to see, because the transmitting of the transcending Christ is so high, far above all.

In order for the church to come into existence, two steps are necessary. First, the materials must be produced, and then these materials need to be formed into a constitution. The transmitting of the transcending Christ is not to produce the church but to form the church. We may use the formation of a nation as an illustration of this. First, the nation needs the people. Over three hundred years ago, many people immigrated to the United States. But these people were not yet a nation. For people to immigrate here was somewhat hard, but for these immigrated people to be formed into a nation was very hard. This needs ability.

Throughout the history of the church, many lovers of the Lord stopped at the first matter, at the producing of the saints, the constituents, but they would not care for the second matter, the constitution and the formation of the church. Today it is the same. Many spiritual giants would not care for the church. They say that if you care for the church, you will have trouble. This is really true. If you only bring people to Christ, everybody will welcome you and highly appraise you. But when you do something to follow the transcending Christ to form the church through His transmitting, you will have trouble.

In the four Gospels, through three and a half years, Christ gathered a group of people. He touched many thousands of people, even feeding five thousand at one time. But eventually He gained only one hundred twenty (Acts 1:15). These one hundred twenty were the produce of the Father's choosing, of the Son's redeeming, and of the Spirit's sealing. In the book of Acts, they were ready to be something, but even they themselves did not know what to be. They waited for seven weeks, from the day of resurrection to the day of Pentecost. On the day of Pentecost, the transcending Christ transmitted His transcending power to these one hundred twenty.

On the day of Pentecost, Peter became different from the way he had his being in the four Gospels. In Matthew 16, he spoke something very high (v. 16), but he spoke mostly in a nonsensical way in the Gospels (Matt. 16:22-23; 17:4-5, 24-27; John 13:6-10). But in Acts, Peter became right-side up. On the day of Pentecost, the transcending Christ transmitted His transcending power into the one hundred twenty and they became the church. So in Acts 2 it was not Peter standing alone to speak; it was Peter standing with the eleven (v. 14). The eleven spoke with him. That indicated it was not one person speaking but the church speaking, so the power was there.

Throughout the history of the church and even today, not many would care for the church. Christ said that He would come quickly, but He does not come quickly according to the way that many Christians think. Without the church being built up, how could Christ come back? This is why seventy years ago, the Lord did something with Brother Nee to take care of the church. This is what is called "the recovery." The taking care of the church had been lost and missed for centuries. But on this earth a young man named Watchman Nee was raised up by the transcending Christ. When he stood up in China, all things rose up against him. Today it is the same. We are still encountering Hades, the earth, the air, and the evil one, who would even go to the third heaven.

All of us need to see this. This is why we need Paul's prayer for the Father to give us a spirit of wisdom with the capacity to understand, to comprehend, and a spirit of revelation with the view. In order to have the view, we need the light. The eyes of our heart need to be enlightened that we may see three things: God's calling, God's inheritance, and God's power. We need to see not only the power but also the surpassing greatness of the power that operated in Christ to raise Him from Hades through the earth, through the air, and through the third heaven to the top of the universe, in order that He might transmit there all that He has obtained and attained to His chosen, redeemed, transformed, prepared people to form them into the church.

CONCLUDING NOTES TO CHAPTER FOUR

1. The triune dispensing of the Father, the Son, and the Spirit in the Father's choosing and predestinating, in the Son's redemption and transformation, and in the Spirit's sealing and pledging issues in bringing forth God's many sons, in producing a heritage of worth to God, and in the transfiguration, glorification, of the regenerated and transformed saints, which is the participation in God's sonship to the fullest. Such a triune dispensing unveils the rich details of the Triune God's dispensing. Yet it has not been consummated to its highest degree. It is the transmitting of the transcending Christ that consummates the divine dispensing to its highest degree. The dispensing of the processed Triune God has issued in the many sons of God, in the heritage of worth to God, and in our fullest participation in the divine sonship, but it has not yet issued in the church, in the Body of Christ. It is the transcending transmission of Christ that issues finally in the church as the Body of Christ. The many sons of God, the heritage of worth, and the divine sonship to its fullest extent are all for the church, the Body of Christ. Yet there is still the need of a consummation. The transcending Christ's transmission fulfills this consummation.

Since the transcending Christ is the embodiment of the Triune God, His transcending transmission includes all the rich dispensing of the Triune God. The Triune God's threefold dispensing is included in the transmission of the transcending Christ and is completed and consummated in the all-inclusive transmission of the transcending Christ.

2. Such an all-inclusive transmission brings us into the union not only with the incarnated and crucified Christ but also with the resurrected and transcending Christ. In union with this transcending Christ, we have surpassed all the negative things and transcended above them all. The incarnated and crucified Christ has brought God to man and has accomplished an eternal redemption for us. But the power of Hades and the rule, authority, power, and lordship in the air are still the frustration to the God-chosen people in their participation in what Christ has done for them in His new covenant. Through Christ's resurrection and ascension, Christ has conquered the power of Hades and surpassed and transcended above all the power of darkness in the air. In union with such a Christ, we are participating all the time in all His success in His resurrection and ascension.

3. The transcending Christ's transmission also brings us into Christ's heavenly ministry in His twelve statuses, as listed above, which He has attained and obtained in His ascension. What a rich source of the bountiful supply into which Christ's transcending transmission has brought us!

Chapter Five

THE CHURCH

Scripture Reading: Eph. 1:22
Hymns: #852, #203

OUTLINE

I. Since the transmitting of the transcending Christ includes all the triune dispensing, it is the total continuation of the dispensing of the Divine Trinity—Eph. 1:19-22a:
  A. The three aspects of the dispensing of the Divine Trinity produce the components of the church, the Body of Christ.
  B. The transmitting of the transcending Christ is the total consummation, to continue the dispensing of the Divine Trinity for the continual and permanent supply to the church, the Body of Christ.
II. The transmitting of the transcending Christ is to transfuse into the church, the Body of Christ, what the Triune God has accomplished, attained, and obtained in Christ:
  A. This is not only for producing the church but also for growing, establishing, and building up the church.
  B. This function is local for the universal Body of Christ and universal for the local churches.
III. The church—Eph. 1:22b:
  A. It is not merely the redeemed, called-out people of God gathering together, as denoted by the Greek word *ekklesia.*
  B. It is also, even more, the organic constitution issued out from the element and essence of the

Triune God into the regenerated believers in Christ that they may be an organism to express the processed Triune God as the Body of Christ:

1. Such a church is universal, but it is to be expressed locally.
2. Though there are many churches locally, yet they are still one Body universally.
3. In nature it is universal; in practice it is local.
4. In business affairs the local churches are different from one another, but in testimony all are identical, like the seven lampstands being indiscernible—Rev. 1:20b.
5. The local churches may be distinct but they should not be divided.
6. Any kind of division damages both the Body and its local expressions.
7. To keep the unique oneness of the one Body in all the local churches is vital, and it safeguards the believers from being led astray.

For this message I would like us to read Ephesians 1:15-23: "Therefore I also, having heard of the faith in the Lord Jesus which is among you and your love to all the saints, do not cease giving thanks for you, making mention of you in my prayers, that the God of our Lord Jesus Christ, the Father of glory, may give to you a spirit of wisdom and revelation in the full knowledge of Him, the eyes of your heart having been enlightened, that you may know what is the hope of His calling, and what are the riches of the glory of His inheritance in the saints, and what is the surpassing greatness of His power toward us who believe, according to the operation of the might of His strength, which He caused to operate in Christ in raising Him from the dead and seating Him at His right hand in the heavenlies, far above all rule and authority and power and lordship and every name that is named not only in this age but also in that which is to come; and He subjected all things under His feet and gave Him to be Head over all things to the church, which is His Body, the fullness of the One who fills all in all."

PRAYING FOR A SPIRIT OF WISDOM AND REVELATION THAT THE EYES OF OUR HEART MAY BE ENLIGHTENED

Paul prayed that we would have a spirit of wisdom and revelation. I want to stress this one point. The book of Ephesians has really become a treasure to many Bible students and teachers, yet very few have seen the intrinsic contents of this prayer in Ephesians 1. The Lord Jesus prayed a great prayer in John 17 concerning His Body in His oneness. The prayer by the apostle Paul in Ephesians 1 should be counted as second to the Lord's prayer in John 17. These are two great prayers. A number of believers may have seen something of the oneness prayed for by the Lord Jesus in John 17, yet not many have seen something in this prayer by the great apostle, Paul.

Paul's prayer is centered on a spirit, our spirit, to be a spirit of wisdom and revelation. Wisdom is for us to have the way to understand, and revelation is the very view for us to see. On the one hand, we need the wisdom to understand, yet we still need the view to see. If we do not see anything, there is nothing for us to understand. First, we have to see the divine view. Through the fellowship in this book, we have seen a view; a view has been opened up. The curtain has been taken away.

We have a clear sky, a clear view, in front of us, yet we also need the wisdom to understand. Nearly all of Ephesians 1 is one sentence in Greek. Chapter two begins with the word *and*. This indicates that the long sentence in chapter one is not finished yet. What Paul said is really hard for us to understand (2 Pet. 3:15-16), so we need the wisdom. This is why I put out the concluding notes at the end of each of the previous four chapters. We should spend some time to get into these notes.

We need to pray, "O Lord, give us a spirit of wisdom and revelation." We have a spirit, but we need a kind of anointing from God to make our spirit a gift from Him. We all have a spirit, but our spirit is not so keen. Instead, it is dull. Thus, we need something from the very inspiring, enlightening God to make our spirit a new gift to us, full of revelation to see God's economy and full of wisdom for us to understand His economy. We need to see and understand God's economy, which is carried out by His divine threefold dispensing to result in the many sons, in the heritage as a treasure to God, and in the glorification of the saints. The many sons, the heritage to God, and the glorification of the saints all come out of God's divine dispensing. How we need the revelation to see this and the wisdom to know this!

Regretfully, many Christians deny that we have a spirit, yet Paul prayed that the Father may give to us a spirit. This is not the Holy Spirit but the human spirit. Paul did not pray that we would have a spirit of power, the kind of so-called power the Pentecostals stress. Power is not what we need. Christ is what we need. We need the wisdom to understand and the view as a revelation for us to see. We need the eyes of our heart to be enlightened. Have we ever heard that our heart has eyes? Our spirit needs the wisdom and revelation, and our heart's two eyes need the enlightenment. We have eyes, but we may have no sight and no light. Without the enlightenment of the divine light, we cannot see.

Paul prayed that the eyes of our heart would be enlightened that we may know three things. The first thing is the hope of God's calling. The second thing is the riches of the glory of God's inheritance in the saints. That means God in His economy through His dispensing will get an inheritance, a heritage of worth, and this heritage will be full of glory. The riches of this glory are unsearchable. Paul also prayed that we would know the great surpassing power that operated in Christ, which is toward us. This is the power that raised up Christ from the dead, from Hades, that seated Christ above all things in the heavens, that subjected all things under His feet, and that gave Him to be Head over all things to the church. This is not common teaching. This is why I have the burden to stress that we all need to have this prayer. We should pray, "Lord, in these days in which You are moving in Your recovery on this earth, I need a spirit of wisdom and of revelation. Lord, give me such a spirit as a great gift."

THE INTRINSIC SIGNIFICANCE OF THE CHURCH

I have spoken on the church many times throughout the past sixty years. When I first began to speak on the church, the standard was too low, but thank God that my speaking on the church has been all the time going up. We need to see what the church is. These messages in this book are of the highest standard because they reveal that the church is the issue of the dispensing of the processed Trinity and the transmitting of the transcending Christ. The church is the issue of God. When God issues out, He becomes the church. The church is the surplus of God.

All of us need to be impressed with the revelation of the church in hymn #203. I wrote this hymn in 1963. During that time I realized there was a shortage of hymns on the deeper truths. This hymn says:

1 In the bosom of the Father,
    Ere the ages had begun,
  Thou wast in the Father's glory,
    God's unique begotten Son.

When to us the Father gave Thee,
Thou in person wast the same,
All the fullness of the Father
In the Spirit to proclaim.

2 By Thy death and resurrection,
Thou wast made God's firstborn Son;
By Thy life to us imparting,
Was Thy duplication done.
We, in Thee regenerated,
Many sons to God became;
Truly as Thy many brethren,
We are as Thyself the same.

3 Once Thou wast the only grain, Lord,
Falling to the earth to die,
That thru death and resurrection
Thou in life may multiply.
We were brought forth in Thy nature
And the many grains became;
As one loaf we all are blended,
All Thy fulness to proclaim.

4 We're Thy total reproduction,
Thy dear Body and Thy Bride,
Thine expression and Thy fulness,
For Thee ever to abide.
We are Thy continuation,
Thy life-increase and Thy spread,
Thy full growth and Thy rich surplus,
One with Thee, our glorious Head.

We must pay our full attention to stanza 4 of this hymn.
This stanza reveals that the church is God's total reproduction, God's dear Body, God's bride, God's expression, God's
fullness, God's continuation, God's life-increase, God's spread,
God's full growth, and God's rich surplus. We may have sung

this hymn many times without any impression of its significance. Stanza 4 of hymn #203 tells us what the church is. Have
we ever considered that as the church we are God's total
reproduction, God's continuation, and God's rich surplus? This
is why we should pray, "Lord, give me a spirit of wisdom and
revelation to sing such a song." We need to read and sing this
song prayerfully until we really see what the church is in its
highest sense. The church is the total reproduction of God!

My burden is not to merely teach us the Bible but to
present us a view so that we can really see what the church
is. The view of the church over these many centuries has
been made very dim. Those who do not see anything at all
say that the church is a physical building. The Brethren
strongly pointed out that the church is not a physical building
but the gathering of God's called-out ones. This is according
to the denotation of the Greek word *ekklesia*. But this still
is not the intrinsic significance of the church. The intrinsic
significance of the church, from the entire New Testament,
is that the church is God's total reproduction, God's continuation, God's increase, God's full growth, and God's rich
surplus. We all should declare, "We are the total reproduction
of God! We are God's continuation! We are God's increase!
We are God's full growth! We are God's rich surplus!" We
may be able to say that we are God's expression, but have
we ever considered that we are God's continuation?

You may wonder where I learned all these things. Years
ago Brother Nee told me face to face that we, the church, are
God's duplication, God's reproduction, and God's continuation.
Without us, God has no continuation. Brother Nee also told
me that we are God's increase and God's full growth, so we
are God's surplus. Such a high vision of the church needs us
to pray, "Lord, give us a spirit of wisdom and revelation to
see and to know what Your church is." We may have heard
that the church is the Body of Christ for the expression of
God. But we still do not know the intrinsic denotation of this
until we see that the church is God's reproduction. The church
is God's xerox copy.

How could the church be the reproduction of God, the
continuation of God? How could the church be the full growth,

increase, and surplus of God? The church can be all these things by the divine dispensing of the Divine Trinity and by the heavenly transmitting of the transcending Christ. We should not say that the transmitting equals the dispensing. That is not right. But we can say that the transmitting comprises, includes, the dispensing. We have to be impressed that the transmitting is crucial but it is not as basic as dispensing. The Father's dispensing, the Son's dispensing, and the Spirit's dispensing are very basic. By, through, and with this threefold, triune dispensing many regenerated sons of God are produced and transformed into a treasure, becoming the heritage to God as God's personal, private possession. Also, the consummation of the processed Triune God as the compound, all-inclusive, indwelling Spirit seals this heritage of God. This sealing is not once for all but is still going on with its spreading effect to saturate and soak the regenerated sons and transformed treasures to make them God in life and nature but not in the Godhead.

But thus far, there has been only the producing of the materials, the components, the constituents, to constitute the Body of Christ. The materials are here, but the formation has not yet taken place. So there is the need of the transmitting of the transcending Christ from the heavens, in the heavens, and with the heavens. The church was formed by the transmitting of the transcending Christ from the heavens, in the heavens, and with the heavens. This is a great thing.

Concerning Christ and the church, there were three great things: incarnation, resurrection, and Pentecost. In incarnation the very God became a man, and this man in resurrection became a life-giving Spirit. On the day of Pentecost, something marvelous took place in the universe. There was the blowing of a rushing violent wind (Acts 2:2), and the church was formed. God became a man, this man became the life-giving Spirit, and this life-giving Spirit brought in the formation of the church, the constitution of the Body of Christ. Now we have a Savior, we have an all-inclusive, consummated Spirit who is the reality of Christ, and this Christ is the very embodiment of the Triune God. Eventually, on the day of Pentecost, He poured out Himself upon all His components to make them one church, one Body. We need a spirit of wisdom to understand to this extent, and we need a spirit of revelation to see to this high standard.

9. Dear saints, the church is the organism of the Triune God. It is not an organization, but an organism, and this organism is the organic Body of Christ. A wooden stand is an organization because it is a mere composition of lifeless materials. But our body is organic, full of life. The church is not an organization nor is it like an inorganic robot. The church is the organic Body of Christ.

6. Also, such a church is God's house. This means the church is God's household, God's family (Eph. 2:19). This is fully unveiled in 1 Timothy 3:15, where Paul told Timothy that the church is the house of the living God. Such a church as the house of God, as the family of God, is the manifestation of God in the flesh (v. 16). The church is not only the house as the household, the family, but also the house as a dwelling place. God has a family on this earth, and He is not homeless. His family becomes His dwelling place. He dwells in you, He dwells in me, and He dwells in all of us, the regenerated sons of God.

Ephesians 2:22 tells us that He makes His habitation in our spirit. The spirit of wisdom and the spirit of revelation eventually becomes God's dwelling place. In the United States there is a motel called "Travelodge." The church is not God's travel lodge but God's permanent lodge on this earth. On the day of Pentecost, something great took place. In the entire universe, God secured a lodge. What a great thing it is that today on the earth God has a lodge, a home, a dwelling place! Fifty or sixty years ago, I was teaching the saints about the church. I told them a number of things about the church, but if you ask me to speak on these matters today, I have no burden. My burden today is to tell you that the church is God's lodge!

THE NEED TO SEE THE ONE CHURCH, THE ONE BODY OF CHRIST

Why has there been turmoil among us? I had a twenty-five-year relationship with Brother Nee. For eighteen years

I was with him shoulder to shoulder. I saw what happened to him. Nearly every seven years there was a turmoil. Why? Because those involved in the turmoil did not see what the church is. All the problems of the church today are due to the ignorance concerning the Body of Christ.

Some might like to talk about the practice of foot-washing. Every time they set up the Lord's table, they insist on the practice of foot washing. When I was young in the Lord, I insisted on baptism by immersion. That was my favorite topic for debate, but I have no heart for things like this anymore. There are so many debates concerning baptism. Should we use fresh water or salt water? Should it be in a lake, a river, or a baptistery? Some think that you cannot follow Jesus to the uttermost unless you go to the Jordan River where Jesus was baptized. But no one knows the very spot where Jesus was baptized. Should we baptize in warm water or cold water? Do we immerse once, twice, or three times? There is no end to these kinds of arguments.

We need to forget about all of these minor things and see what the church is. The church is the organism of the Triune God. The church is the organic Body of Christ, which is God's family, God's household, God's folks becoming His home, His dwelling place. There is no need to argue about any doctrinal matters or practices. We just need to see and know that the church is God's total reproduction, God's continuation, God's full growth, God's increase, God's rich surplus, and this surplus today is the organism of the Triune God, the organic Body of Christ, which is the family, the folks of God becoming His dwelling place on this earth. Today God not only is with us, with the church, but also has made us His dwelling place.

Some like to talk about the distinction between the universal church and the local churches. Even such a thing is not worthwhile of arguing about. God's house, the Body of Christ, is just one. Some say that the church is local and the work is regional. We need to forget about all these things. We need to see that we are one church. Some may say that the saints in Taipei cannot meet with the saints in Anaheim, so apparently in practice there are two churches—one in Anaheim and one in Taipei. Actually, today in the Lord's recovery there are over twelve hundred churches, but all of these churches are parts of the one church, the one Body of Christ. On this earth there is the element of space and the element of time. But with God there is no space element and no time element. In His eyes in the whole universe there is one church.

The final point of my burden in this chapter is that we should not consider just our church in our city. We have to consider God's church in the universe. We may wonder how to practice this, but we should not worry about this. Now we are in a city, and we simply need to come together to meet. We can say we are a local church, but we are not separated from the church of God. We are just a part of the church of God.

If you have received the gift of a spirit of wisdom and of revelation, you will see that the church is just one. In the eyes of God, all the local churches are just one. When you live in a certain town, you meet with the saints in that town. You are still a part of the one church of God. You may say, "I'm burdened to build up the church in my locality." You are burdened, but God is not so burdened. He is burdened to build up His church, the one church of God.

When the church was first formed, it was very normal. But after a short while, Satan came in and did something to damage the one Body of Christ, the one church of God. Satan worked to such an extent to form the Catholic Church. The word catholic means universally one. In a sense this is not bad. All the saints are one church. We are all catholic, but the Catholic Church is under a pope. Under the pope are the cardinals, who are the cabinet members of the papal government. Then under the cardinals are the archbishops, the bishops, and the priests. This forms a hierarchy to control people. That damaged the Body of Christ to the uttermost for ten centuries, from about A.D. 500 to 1500.

Then Martin Luther was raised up in the Reformation. He left the Catholic Church, but he did not take care of the truth concerning the church. Instead, he helped the Germans to form the state church, the church of a nation. Eventually, other state churches were formed in the Scandinavian countries and in England. Today there is the Church of England, and the queen of England is the head of the Anglican church, the Episcopalian church.

Some pursuers and lovers of Christ did not agree with the Catholic Church or the state churches, so they invented the private churches. Today there are private churches such as the Baptist church, practicing baptism by immersion, and the Presbyterian church, practicing the government of the church through the presbytery.

Eventually, the Brethren rose up in England, and they stressed that the church should not be under anyone's control. The church must be free. They were free to such an extent that they established local churches on streets. These were not city churches but street churches. Not long after the Brethren were raised up, they were divided into hundreds of divisions. I know of one case where a group of them divided over whether to have a piano or an organ in their services. Thus, one group became a "piano church," and the other became an "organ church."

Today there are also the Pentecostals who care only for speaking in tongues and miraculous gifts, not for God's desire to have His one church. Many of them do not care whether their speaking in tongues is real or false. Other seekers of Christ take the excuse that they do not like to be under any man. They only want to be under the Holy Spirit. If I do not want to be under you and you do not want to be under me, we cannot have a church life. Instead, each of us becomes a "church." Today there is much division and confusion among the Lord's children. There are many Chinese churches such as the Church of Taiwan in Anaheim and the Taiwan Church of the Gospel. People are too free to set up divisions. It seems that establishing a church is easier than establishing a restaurant.

We need to have a church life, so we need to be clear about today's situation. Our constitution is the Bible. We must come back to our constitution and check everything of today's situation with what the Bible says. We must come back to the Bible and see what the Bible says about the church. God's economy is not for the purpose of having only individual

believers to be saved, to be spiritual, and then to go to heaven.
This is not God's economy. This is the teaching of fallen
Christianity. The Bible tells us God has a desire, and He has
made an economy to dispense Himself into His chosen people
and make His chosen people His many sons. Then He
transforms them into His treasure and seals them with His
life element unto the redemption of their body. Through the
transcending Christ's transmitting, He brings them together
to make them one church. This is why we say that there is
the need of a recovery of the proper church life according to
God's economy.

Praise the Lord and thank the Lord that we have seen
the light to this extent, and we have been brought into the
Lord's recovery. But regretfully, our seeing is not that high.
Our sight is not up to the standard. We are still merely for
our local church in our city. This is wrong. None of us should
be only for our church in our city. We are here for God's
church in the universe. Every local expression, every local
church, should be the same to us. If I am in Anaheim, I
surely should meet, worship, serve, and work in the church
in Anaheim. Next year I may go to Taipei. Then after another
month, I may go to another place. Every church is my church
because that is God's church. There are no regional differ-
ences. To think that a certain region is my region for my
work is wrong. Christ has only one Body.

We need a spirit of wisdom and revelation with the eyes
of our heart being enlightened to see God's vision and to
know God's economy in His wisdom. The center of God's
economy is His desire to have many sons constituted through
transformation into one Body, which is the church to be
expressed on this earth in many localities as local expressions, local churches, and all these local churches are one
church. 5-27-03 ST, DH, KR, MB, BM, David C,
B+SN, Rusty H.

CHAPTER SIX

THE BODY OF CHRIST

Scripture Reading: Eph. 1:23

OUTLINE

I. It is the intrinsic significance of the church.

II. It is the divine constitution of the Triune God with the believers in Christ—Eph. 4:4-6.

III. It is a mingling of divinity with humanity.

IV. It is an organism, both divine and human, to express Christ.

V. It is the fullness of the all-inclusive Christ, the One who fills all in all—Eph. 1:23:

    A. Fullness is the issue of the riches of Christ—Eph. 3:8.

    B. Fullness is the expression of the inner riches.

VI. Such an organic Body is:

    A. Undivided and indivisible as Christ is—1 Cor. 1:13a.

    B. Not autonomous.

VII. This unique Body of Christ is expressed in many local churches—Rev. 1:11:

    A. In the divine oneness as it is with the Triune God—John 17:11, 21, 23.

    B. In the divine nature, element, essence, expression, function, and testimony.

    C. Kept by the believers in the practical one accord—Acts 1:14; 2:46; 4:24; 5:12; 15:25; Rom. 15:6.

VIII. The divine oneness of the Body of Christ should be kept both in the local churches as the local expressions of the Body and in the universal source and substance.

IX. This genuine oneness of the Body of Christ is one

crucial point of the Lord's recovery in the consummating age.

X. All the problems of the church today are due to the ignorance concerning the Body of Christ.

I believe that in the past five chapters we have seen God's economy. We have also seen that the way to carry out the Triune God's economy is by His threefold dispensing plus Christ's onefold transmitting. These two things work together. The threefold dispensing produces the many sons and transforms them into God's heritage of worth. This transformation will go on and on through the Spirit's continual sealing until one day the result will come out. That result will be the transfiguration of our vile body, which will bring all of us into God's glory. This is the issue of the triune dispensing to produce the materials for the building up of the church, the Body of Christ.

Then the church comes into existence through the transcending Christ's transcending transmission, and this transmission took place on the day of Pentecost. In the history of the universe, such a marvelous thing took place. Suddenly in one day, the church as the Body of Christ came into being. Now the church, the Body of Christ, is here. Today we are enjoying Him in His Body, His church.

[margin handwritten note: Acts 2:33— Jm asc, poured out HÍs Sp. 1 Cor 12:13 bptizd in 1 Sp into 1 Bdy]

THE IMPORTANCE OF THE MINGLED SPIRIT
IN THE BOOK OF EPHESIANS

Before we speak further concerning the Body of Christ, I want to point out something crucial in the book of Ephesians. In each of the six chapters of Ephesians, the human spirit is mentioned. Our human spirit has been regenerated and indwelt by the compound, all-inclusive, consummated Spirit to make this spirit a mingled spirit.

In 1:17 the apostle Paul prayed that the Father would give us such a mingled spirit of wisdom to understand and of revelation to see. We need the revelation and the enlightenment to see the mystery of God's economy. We also need to understand, to apprehend, what we see by the divine wisdom. The economy of God is a real mystery, yet it has been revealed to us. We can see His economy and it is made known to us so that we can receive it, understand it, apprehend it, and participate in it.

Ephesians 2:22 says that all the believers are being built together to be God's habitation in spirit. God needs a dwelling place, not just in the heavens but on the earth, and this dwelling place must be organic in our spirit. This spirit is not the dweller; rather, it is the dwelling place. God mingled Himself with our spirit, and our spirit is His dwelling place. God is here dwelling in us. He is in our spirit, which is His resting place.

Ephesians 3:5 tells us that the economy of God, which is so mysterious, has been unveiled to the apostles and the prophets in their spirit. This revelation was given not in their mind but in their spirit. If we are going to understand, to realize, the reality of God's mysterious economy, we must learn to discern our spirit from our soul (Heb. 4:12). We should not be bothered by our soul. We should not be troubled, complicated, and perplexed by our mind. Instead, we should always turn to our spirit where we can meet the divine Spirit. In our mingled spirit, we have the capacity to see the mystery of God's economy, to understand it, to apprehend it, and to receive it and retain it as our portion.

Ephesians 4:23 says that we have to be renewed in the spirit of our mind. Our spirit can become the spirit of our mind. Actually, the fallen mind is a bad thing. There are a number of bad things within us, and the leading one is our mind. We have to hate our mind. When we exercise our mind too much, we get ourselves "hung on a tree" like Absalom (2 Sam. 18:9-10). But we have the best thing in us, that is, our spirit. This thing, our spirit, can even go into our mind. Our spirit can come into our mind, subdue it, take it over, and occupy it. It can then become the spirit of our mind. Then we have a wonderful mind, a mind that has the spirit within it. It is by this spirit of the mind that we are renewed every day into the image of our Creator (Col. 3:10). Day by day we are being renewed by the spirit who is taking over our mind. It is in this way that we are transformed and conformed to the image of our Creator.

Ephesians 5:18 tells us not to be drunk with wine, that is, not to be filled in our physical body with wine. Instead, we should be filled in our spirit. Our spirit needs to be filled with the processed Triune God, with the transcending Christ, with the consummated Spirit. Then we will be full of praise, singing and speaking one to another (vv. 19-20). The melodies, the songs, are not only good for singing but also good for speaking. As we speak to one another in psalms, hymns, and spiritual songs, as we are praising God, we will spontaneously be submissive to one another (v. 21). The wives will be submissive to the husbands, and the husbands will love the wives (vv. 22, 25). Then we will have the proper church life, full of submission and full of praising to the Triune God, with no quarreling, no murmuring, and no complaining.

Ephesians 6 tells us something further. On the one hand, the church life is a praising life and a submitting life; at the same time it is also a fighting life. While we are praising and submitting to one another, the enemy is here fighting, so we have to fight against him by prayer. Verse 18 says that whenever we pray, we should pray in our spirit, not in our mind. If we are going to walk, we need to use our feet. No one can walk by his nose. Even for someone to walk on his hands is awkward. To walk by our feet is the right way. In the same way, we should not pray merely by our mind. We must pray by our spirit and in our spirit.

Our spirit mingled with the Spirit has been mentioned six times in the book of Ephesians. This indicates that to know God's economy, to receive His dispensing, and to participate in Christ's transmission, we must know, we must use, and we must exercise our spirit. We should not be persons in our mind but persons in our spirit.

We may be exercising our spirit to worship the Lord at His table, but afterward we may immediately turn to our mind. The wife may begin to think about how badly her husband treated her the previous evening. Then her emotion gets stirred up and her will makes a decision to threaten him. This is the result of her not exercising her spirit. She should not think about her husband. Instead, she should praise the Lord in the spirit and pray in the spirit. If we do this, we will be victorious. When we exercise our mind in an independent way, we are defeated. When we turn back to our spirit, we become the victor.

We should not consider or talk about the things of the church life by our mind. If we exercise our mind to consider and speak of the church life, we will say that the elders are not that good. We will also say that the old saints and the young people are not good and that the children are naughty. Eventually, to our mind nothing is good in the church life. Even when we are praying, a negative thought may come into our mind that a certain brother is not so good. Quite often in our good prayer, we are stopped by just one thought. Right away we have to shout, "Praise the Lord! Jesus is Victor!" We need to chase away the enemy in our mind and continue to pray. Sometimes we may have to rise up from our knees and say, "Satan, get away! Praise the Lord! Lord, You are the Victor!"

If we have any problem concerning the church, we must exercise our spirit to pray. Then we will have the vision to see and the wisdom to understand. Then we will understand why there is the need of the onefold transmission to follow the threefold dispensing of the Divine Trinity. We will see that this transmission is by the One who transcended from Hades through the earth, through the air, and through the third heaven to become higher than the heavens.

THE CHURCH BEING GOD'S GOAL
AND THE TARGET OF THE ENEMY

There is the need of such a transmission, because there are layers of opposition. In Hades there is opposition. On this earth there is opposition. In the air there is opposition. There is opposition from the evil one, who would even go to the third heaven. Mainly all this opposition is against the church. If we would speak only about the threefold dispensing, the triune dispensing, everyone would think this is wonderful, but once we speak about the church, opposition rises up. This is because the church is God's goal.

When I first came to this country, I was warmly welcomed. In 1964 I was invited to speak to a group of people in Dallas. I was there for a week of conference meetings. My host and hostess exhorted me to speak only on Christ and not touch the church. They said that if I touched the church, no one would come the next day. At the end of this week, I realized that the Lord was burdened for me to speak on the church, so I made a strong resolution to do it. Before I spoke, I asked them to read Romans 12. By reading Romans 12 the host and the hostess realized that I would speak on the church, so they dropped their heads. That bothered the congregation. But there was a young man there by the name of Benson Phillips. Eventually, through that whole week, he was and still is the unique one caught by the Lord. So actually, I spent the whole week there just to catch him. After he came in, he took the lead among the saints in Texas, and now he has been sent to Russia.

Would you speak on the church? It is a battle to touch the church, to speak about the church. The church is the goal of God, and the church is the very target of the enemy. Throughout my over sixty years of ministry, I have been warned not to speak about the church. I was advised to just speak concerning the riches of Christ. The church is a bothering matter.

THE NEED TO SEE THE ONE BODY, THE ONE CHURCH OF GOD

Look at today's situation with the thousands of divisions among the Lord's people. There is a "church market" full of division and confusion. In Anaheim there is a division called the Church of Taiwan in Anaheim. In my home town of Chefoo in mainland China, there was a division called the Church of England in China. Logically, the Church of England should be in England, and the Church of Taiwan should be in Taiwan. What confusion this is! Today there are not only divisions but also confusion. People have argued and have been divided over whether to have wine or grape juice at the Lord's table. They have also been divided over what kind of bread to use at the Lord's table.

In the recent past, there was a different teaching among us which said that the local church should be autonomous. If we receive such a teaching, this means that we have not seen that the church is the Body of Christ. Can any part of our physical body be autonomous? If the various parts of our body were autonomous, this would mean that our body was cut into pieces. How could we make our blood circulation autonomous? The circulation of our blood is throughout our entire body. In the same way, no part of the Body of Christ can be autonomous.

But some may argue by saying, "Brother Lee, didn't you say that the administration of the churches should be local and independent?" I may have said that many years ago, but if you asked me to repeat such a saying today, I would not do it. We may think that the local churches are independent, but in the Bible I cannot find the thought of independence. Who is independent from whom in the Body of Christ? Is the church in Anaheim independent from the church in Dallas? The word *independence* should not be brought in when we are speaking about the Body of Christ. We are not independent. Instead, we all are dependent on one another. The church in Anaheim depends upon the church in Fullerton, and the church in Fullerton depends upon the church in Anaheim. We are not independent. We are one Body. Are the churches in Taiwan independent from the churches in America? In the Body of Christ, this cannot be.

The churches may be different in their business affairs, but even in this matter they should not claim that they are independent. What if the church in Anaheim made a decision to meet at two o'clock in the morning? The leading ones there may claim that the local church has its own jurisdiction and that no one can interfere with them. But the church in Santa Ana may ask, "Why have you brothers in Anaheim made such a decision to meet at two o'clock in the morning?" The brothers in Anaheim may say that those in Santa Ana should not interfere with them, that this is not their business, and that the church in Anaheim is independent and has its own jurisdiction. But to meet at two o'clock in the morning is peculiar and odd to the uttermost. In this matter the church in Anaheim needs the helpful advice from the church in Santa Ana. It is not wise to make a decision to meet at two o'clock in the morning. This illustration shows that we need the advice and help from the other churches even in business affairs and practical things.

There are many times when I am adjusted in my fellowship with the co-workers. The brothers may remind me of something that would change our consideration in certain matters. In this particular conference, we brothers came together before the meetings to pray and fellowship about certain things. Some of the brothers asked me whether or not we needed to meet before the Lord's table meeting, since this meeting would be a little earlier. We felt that there would be no need for us to come together before this meeting. This is the fellowship of the Body. I should not say to the brothers, "This conference is my conference. This is not your business. Don't interfere with my jurisdiction." This would be terrible. But this is actually the practice in some places—if not outwardly, at least inwardly.

If we claim to be independent, we damage ourselves. We should never forget that God has only one church. The church in Anaheim is just a small part of the church of God. We should not think that there is the church of God plus the church in Anaheim. When we speak of the church of God, we imply the local church. Through the years I have learned the following lesson. The more we honor the uniqueness of the church, the more blessings we will receive. The church in which you are meeting today may be in Spokane or in Anaheim, but we have to remember that these are just parts of the church. They are not independent. We are dependent upon one another. All the churches need the help of the other churches because we are one Body. We have to see the Body.

Because we are on this earth, we are limited by time and space, and we have many business affairs. The saints in Anaheim and the saints in San Francisco and Fresno cannot meet together often. This is impossible because of the inconvenience of distance. They need to have their own particular activities. The church in Fresno may decide to rent a small hall, whereas the church in Anaheim meets in a big hall. This is altogether according to the practical need. But this does not indicate any division, separation, or independence.

When all the churches come together for a conference, those who are coming from another city may not function in the conference. They may think, "This is not my home church." As a result, they would not function. But certain brothers who live in the locality where the conference is held may function frequently because they think, "This is my home church." Dear saints, this is wrong. The Lord has only one Body. The church of God is only one. In 1 Corinthians 10:32 Paul spoke of three categories of people on this earth: the Jews, God's chosen people; the Greeks, the unbelieving Gentiles; and the church of God, a composition of the believers in Christ. The church is uniquely one on this earth. If I go to London, I should not consider that I am from the United States and that this is their church. I should not consider that I am a guest and they are the host, that they have their jurisdiction and that I have no concern in the church there. This is wrong. I should consider that I am a member of the church of God, which is universal and sometimes local. It is okay to say *sometimes* but not *all times*.

Two thousand years ago, the communication and the means of travel were not as convenient as they are today. Even fifty years ago, it took me forty-eight hours to travel by boat from my home town, Chefoo, to Shanghai. Later, after World War II it took only forty-five minutes to travel this distance by plane. Today the world has become so small. I am so glad that the world situation is tending this way. This is for our experience of the genuine oneness of the Body of Christ. How can we keep ourselves independent and keep our so-called jurisdiction, saying, "This is my city. This is my country. This is my region"? In today's world and in today's recovery, we cannot and should not do this.

In 1963 I told the saints that the international trade and commerce would turn from the Atlantic to the Pacific. This is why I chose Los Angeles to be my place for the Lord's ministry. Now we can see that there is much more traffic for commerce on the Pacific than on the Atlantic. The world has changed, so we should not keep ourselves in a backward state. If we are going to have the Lord's blessing, we must be one in all the parts of the recovery.

The Lord Jesus prayed for this in John 17. He prayed to the Father, "That they may be one even as We are" (vv. 11, 21). We should keep the oneness. If we are narrow, independent, and insisting on our jurisdiction in our locality, we will not even be able to be in one accord with others in our locality. Universally, we should be one. Locally, we should be in one accord. Are you expecting to see the Lord's blessing? You must learn the "two-layer lesson." Locally, you must serve with the saints in one accord. Universally, all the churches should be one.

Today's problems in the Lord's recovery are all due to one thing—we have not seen the Body. If we have seen the Body, there is no problem. Then minor things such as whether we use leavened or unleavened bread and wine or grape juice at the Lord's table will not matter. As long as we receive the threefold dispensing of the Father, of the Son, and of the Spirit, everything is okay. As long as we would stay under the transmission of the transcending Christ from the heavens, everything is okay.

THE DAMAGE OF OPINIONS

Opinions are another source of division. In one Lord's table meeting, I saw a situation which illustrates this. In this table meeting, the cup and the bread were covered with a cloth. After a short time, one brother stood up to take off the cloth. His reason was that the elements should be seen in order to display the Lord's death. But later another brother came back to put the cloth back on the elements. His reason for doing this was to protect the bread and the wine from a fly in the meeting. Both of these brothers were bothered with each other. They were opinionated. Could that table have been blessed by the Lord? If the one brother was afraid to receive some sickness through the fly, the wise thing would have been not to say anything or do anything. When the cup came to him, he simply could have not taken it and passed it on to someone else. He should have had no opinion.

I would like to give another illustration to show how opinions can frustrate things. Three brothers were going to take a car from Anaheim to Los Angeles. Before they started, they began to argue about which was the best way to take. They argued with one another for a long time. By that time they would have already arrived in Los Angeles, regardless of what way they had taken. This shows how opinions can delay us.

For over sixty years I have been serving the church and ministering the word to the churches. It has been hard to see a brother who was not opinionated. Anyone who is opinionated does not see the Body. If you check with the brothers who have been working together with me for the past five years here in Anaheim, they can tell you that I never argue with them. If they ask me about their feeling to go somewhere, I will tell them to pray and that if they feel led of the Lord and can be spared, to go. These brothers can tell you that I am not opinionated. Many times the sisters are very opinionated. They may not express their opinions to others, but they will to their husbands. We need to reject our opinions, because they damage the Body of Christ.

I. THE BODY BEING THE INTRINSIC SIGNIFICANCE OF THE CHURCH

We need to see the way Paul presents the Body of Christ in Ephesians 1. Paul said that God raised up Christ, seated Him in the heavens, subjected all things under His feet, and gave Him to be Head over all things to the church. Right away in the following phrase he said, "Which is His Body" (v. 23a). The church is the Body. This indicates that the Body is the church's intrinsic significance. The church without the Body means nothing. In Greek the church is the *ekklesia,* the called-out ones coming together. But the significance of this gathering is the Body.

In the recovery today there are over twelve hundred churches around the globe, yet we all are one Body. If we consider ourselves as individual churches or as individual believers, we are through. We should consider ourselves as one Body. If the parts of our physical body would keep their own jurisdiction and be autonomous, our body would be finished. But thank the Lord that all the members of our physical body are submissive to one another so that our body can act and operate smoothly. Suppose that we wanted to go somewhere and that all the parts of our body agreed except our feet. If the feet could talk, they might say to the other members, "Don't you know that we are tired. You have no love. You don't sympathize with us. You want to go, but we will not go, because we do not have the strength to go." What kind of physical body would this be? In practicality, there would be no body. This is to be "disbodied." Today among the Christians concerning the Body of Christ, it is like this. They are "disbodied."

At least I can testify for myself and for my senior brother, Brother Watchman Nee. We always behaved, acted, and took action in the recovery as one Body. This is why the Lord's recovery could exist on this earth over these past approximately seventy years. We do not have any organization to keep anything, but the recovery is still here. The recovery is still existing and has been kept by the principle of the Body. While I was ministering the word, I often considered Brother Nee. I considered what he spoke; I did not like to speak anything which was contradicting with his ministry. If I had spoken in a contradicting way, where would the recovery be today? We must know the Body.

I would like to say again that the Body is the intrinsic significance of the church. If there were no Body, the church would have no meaning. The church makes no sense without the Body. But hallelujah, there is the Body! Without the Body, the church makes no sense, but with the Body, there is the intrinsic significance of the church.

The transcending Christ is far above all. He is above Hades, above the earth, above the air, and even above the third heaven. This One is transmitting Himself to the church, which is the Body of Him who fills all in all.

What is the difference between the church and the Body? We need to see that the church of God is the frame and the Body of Christ is the organism. We can use an apple tree as an illustration. The tree is the frame, and the apples are the very organic essence of this tree. If you have only the tree, that does not mean much. The tree is for the apples. We do not eat the tree; we eat the apples. Apples come out of the tree. The church is the frame, like the apple tree, and the Body of Christ is the very organic essence of the church, just like the apples are the very organic essence of the apple tree.

These two are one. The church is the frame for existing. The Body of Christ is the very organic contents for people's satisfaction.

We have encountered much opposition due to one thing. We are here not just for the gospel to save souls. We are here to carry out God's eternal economy, with the purpose of gaining a Body for His Son, Christ, and this Body has to be consolidated into the local churches. In this country there have been a number of spiritual giants, but no one would care for the church. They care only for saving souls, but where are those millions of souls today? Where is God's economy? Where is the church for the Body? Where is the "apple tree" and where are the "apples" today? As far as God's economy is concerned, there is very little on this earth for the fulfilling of God's intention according to His heart's desire. But I have the full assurance that the recovery we are taking care of today, by His mercy and grace, is absolutely of the Lord. The strongest evidence of this is the Lord's speaking. Through many years the Lord's oracle on this earth has been and still is in the recovery.

II. THE DIVINE CONSTITUTION OF THE TRIUNE GOD WITH THE BELIEVERS IN CHRIST

The Body of Christ is the divine constitution of the Triune God with the believers in Christ. Ephesians 4:4-6 shows us the constitution of the three divine persons with all His chosen people. So we have the one Body, one Spirit, one Lord, and one God and Father mingled together.

III. A MINGLING OF DIVINITY WITH HUMANITY

The Body of Christ is a mingling of the Divine Trinity with all His chosen human beings. It is a mingling of divinity with humanity.

IV. AN ORGANISM, BOTH DIVINE AND HUMAN, TO EXPRESS CHRIST

The Body of Christ is an organism. On the one hand, it is divine. On the other hand, it is human to express the divine

and human Christ, who is ~~both the complete God and~~ the
~~perfect man.~~

V THE FULLNESS OF THE ALL-INCLUSIVE CHRIST

The Body of Christ is the fullness of the all-inclusive
Christ, the One who fills all in all (Eph. 1:23). In the book
of Ephesians we have these two terms—the *riches of Christ*
and the *fullness of Christ*. The fullness is the issue of the
riches of Christ (3:8) and the ~~expression~~ of these inner riches.
In 1962, I was invited to speak to a group of people in the
Bay Area. My subject was the riches of Christ issuing in His
fullness. They were surprised by this subject.

A number of Christians think that the fullness and the
riches are the same thing. But the fullness is the issue and
the expression of the riches. A tall, husky American brother
has eaten many of the riches of America. All these American
riches have been digested and assimilated by him, and ~~he is~~
now the fullness of ~~Ameri~~ca, the issue and expression of the
riches of America.

We need to be the same with Christ. We should enjoy the
riches of Christ until we become the fullness of Christ. When
we are full of the riches, this fullness overflows. A cup may
have water within it, but we cannot see the water. But if the
cup is filled to the brim with water, it overflows with water.
This overflow is the fullness, the expression, of the water.
We need to be filled with Christ until we overflow with Him.
This overflow is the fullness, and the fullness is the
expression.

VII THE ORGANIC AND UNIQUE BODY OF CHRIST EXPRESSED IN MANY LOCAL CHURCHES

The organic Body is undivided and it is also indivisible
(1 Cor. 1:13a). It is not autonomous. This unique Body of Christ
is expressed in many local churches (Rev. 1:11) in the divine
oneness as it is with the Triune God (John 17:11, 21, 23) and
in the divine nature, element, essence, expression, function, and
testimony. There are many churches, yet they have one divine
nature, one divine element, one divine essence, one divine
expression, one divine function, and one divine testimony

because they are one Body. This is why I say that our troubles are due to not seeing the Body. If we have seen the Body, there will be no problem. The principle and practice of the one Body are kept by the believers in the practical one accord (Acts 1:14; 2:46; 4:24; 5:12; 15:25; Rom. 15:6).

VII. KEEPING THE DIVINE ONENESS OF THE BODY OF CHRIST

The divine oneness of the Body of Christ should be kept both in the local churches as the local expressions of the Body and in the universal source and substance. In every way we should keep the divine oneness of the Body of Christ.

A. ONE CRUCIAL POINT OF THE LORD'S RECOVERY IN THE CONSUMMATING AGE

The genuine oneness of the Body of Christ is one crucial point of the Lord's recovery in this consummating age. The Lord is going to consummate His economy, so to keep the oneness is very crucial.

B. THE IGNORANCE CONCERNING THE BODY OF CHRIST

All the problems of the church today are due to the ignorance concerning the Body of Christ. Among us this ignorance should be absent, and the full knowledge should be present. We need a spirit of wisdom and revelation with the enlightening of the eyes of our heart to see and apprehend the Body of Christ.

CHAPTER SEVEN

A CONCLUDING WORD

I thank the Lord for the rich blessing, even the particular blessing, that He has bestowed upon this conference. Through the ministry and fellowship in this conference, Ephesians 1 has become much more clear to me in three points: first, in the triune dispensing of the Divine Trinity; second, in the unique transmitting of the transcending Christ; and third, in the spirit of wisdom and revelation, through which we can realize and participate in the triune dispensing and the unique transmitting. In these three matters I believe that the Lord will have a way to carry out His economy in this consummated age.

I do look to the Lord that He would show us that His triune dispensing is to produce continuously the materials, components, and constituents of the Body of Christ. After this, there is the need of the transcending Christ's unique transmitting to put all the materials, components, and constituents together to have a constitution, which is the organism of the Triune God, the organic Body of Christ. This is the unique way for us to touch, see, realize, comprehend, and even participate in and enjoy both the constituents and the constitution.

From now on the goal among us for the Lord's recovery should be just to humble ourselves, telling the Lord that we have been very poor in His recovery for many years. We have been distracted in many ways and affected by many things, and have even been to some extent captured by these things. The Lord forgives us, and now His mercy with His grace still takes care of us. I believe that this conference has been a great caring of the Head for us as the Body.

Today the vision among us is very clear. Therefore, we

must forget about the past and forget about what we know and have a new beginning with a renewed practice. We need to pray much for our spirit: "Lord, now I am clear. In such a crucial book as Ephesians, You unveiled to us Your triune dispensing and Your unique transmitting. At the same time You also unveiled to us how much You expect that we all could have a spirit of wisdom and revelation. Thank You, Lord, that You inspired Your apostle Paul to pray for us. While he was ministering to us the threefold dispensing and the unique transmitting, he prayed; he inserted a prayer into his ministry. He prayed for us desperately, that our God as the Father would give to us a spirit of wisdom and revelation."

The divisions and the confusions among God's chosen people did not begin with us. If we read the Acts and the Epistles along with the book of Revelation, we will see a picture, a portrait, of the divisions and confusions that existed even before the end of the first century. Paul was martyred before A.D. 70. Before his martyrdom he wrote 2 Timothy. In that book we can see the confusion and division that existed at that time (1:15; 2:16-18; 3:1-9; 4:3-4, 10, 14-16). Not only so, even in Galatians and Philippians Paul showed us that at his time there were not only divisions but also rivalries. Some brothers were competing against Paul (Gal. 1:6-7; 3:1; 4:13-17; 6:12; Phil. 1:15-18, 28; 2:20-21; 3:2).

The situation that is among us today existed also in Paul's time. I do not think that the degree of trouble in Paul's time was lower than in ours. Today it seems that there is not a person who is doing evil things to the degree that Alexander the coppersmith did evil to the apostle Paul (2 Tim. 4:14). Therefore, we should not be disappointed with the present confusing and dividing situation. Rather, we should be very encouraged and very grateful to the Lord that in such an age He has visited us and brought us into the recovery and has been with us these many years. Furthermore, in this conference the Lord has shown us something further, deeper, higher, and richer in the book of Ephesians. What the Lord has shown us surpassed my expectation.

Through the six chapters in this book we have a clear sky to show us that in the entire universe there is a threefold dispensing of the processed Triune God—not the "raw" God, not the God who was only in His divinity in eternity past, but the Triune God who has been processed to dispense Himself in a threefold way. He came out of eternity with His divinity to enter into humanity, and He was even born of a human virgin. He passed through such an incarnation. What a process it was for Him as the almighty, infinite, eternal God to become a small man, even to lie in a manger and to grow gradually according to the principles of His creation! In His creation God ordained many principles. Human birth takes place according to God's regulation, God's ordination. In His birth as a man He kept all those ordinations, and then He remained in a poor carpenter's home for thirty years. After ministering for three and a half years, He willingly entered into death to visit Hades, and there He overcame death and put down Hades, and He walked out from that place and entered into resurrection. In His resurrection He accomplished a number of things. First, He became the life-giving Spirit (1 Cor. 15:45). Second, He was willing to be born again with His humanity to be the firstborn Son of God, thus opening the gate so that the Father could have many sons with both humanity and divinity (Acts 13:33; Rom. 8:29). According to 1 Peter 1:3, in His birth He begot millions of God's chosen people in His resurrection. Then He, with the Father's divine economy, transcended all the oppositions in the universe. He transcended Hades, the human opposition on the earth, and the evil angelic opposition in the air. He transcended far above all to sit at the right hand of His Father, the Almighty in this universe (Eph. 1:20-21). Not only so, the Father subjected all things under His feet and gave Him a great gift, that is, to be the Head over all things to the church (v. 22). Now, all that He accomplished in His transcending is to the church. The little word *to* in Ephesians 1:22 implies transmission.

All the constituents needed for the constituting of His organic Body were produced in the threefold dispensing of the Divine Trinity. In Christ's unique transmitting, He put all these constituents together to form a Body. This Body is not merely a church as a gathering of called-out believers, but an organic constitution, the organism of the Triune God. This organism is also the unique house of the Triune God (1 Tim. 3:15), and this house is both the household and the dwelling place of God (Eph. 2:19-22). The formation of the church as the Body of Christ was a great event on this earth, and even in the entire universe. The people of the world do not have the ability to see this, but we have the capacity to see it, because we were born of Him and were born into His kingdom (John 1:12-13; 3:5).

People who work in education have found out that in a human being there is a great capacity to learn. Even a three-year-old child can understand many things. There is a hidden capacity in those who were born as human beings. In addition to our human birth, we have experienced a new birth. We must believe that in this new birth there is a hidden capacity. The only thing we need is to develop that hidden capacity. A small child needs a little stirring up to bring out the hidden capacity within him. So Paul prayed that the Father would give the dear saints a spirit of wisdom and revelation. Actually, the wisdom is there already. Paul's prayer was just to stir up the hidden capacity so that we can understand God and His mysterious economy. No doubt the messages in this conference have stirred up our spiritual capacity, which we have by our spiritual birth. This is altogether the mercy of the Lord.

After you read the messages in this book, I would beg you to kneel down and pray: "Lord, I do not need anything today. I only need You. Grant me a favor by stirring up my spiritual capacity which I have from my spiritual birth. Stir up my spirit with wisdom so that I can understand. Lord, forgive me; until today my understanding of You and of the things concerning You has been altogether natural. Thank You that through this conference You have opened the veil to show us something. I am here waiting on You. Lord, day by day grant me a spirit of wisdom and revelation." I would encourage you to pray for this, dear saints, for at least one or two months.

In the past our vision depended too much on our natural concept, and our natural concept has been influenced by the traditional Christianity. It does not care for the capacity to understand God's economy, but it has done much to frustrate us, to distract us, and to bring us into darkness. We have been put into darkness by God's enemy Satan, by the power of darkness. He has caused God's holy Word to become dim without the light we need.

Nevertheless, how I thank the Lord that today the Bible is a shining book to us! The Lord's revelation still remains in His recovery. We need to worship Him for His oracle.

I urge you to go to the Lord with a praying spirit and tell the Lord, "Lord, I need a spirit of wisdom and revelation. I need to see much more of Your triune dispensing. I desire to see, dear Lord, that as the transcending One You are still carrying out a unique transmission." Without this transmission Watchman Nee could not have been raised up. To the great surprise of the missionaries in China, a native Chinese stood up to speak for God. During his ministry Brother Nee was very much opposed, but no opposition ever overcame him. This was due to the transmitting of the transcending Christ.

In this transmitting there is the transcending power. This power raised Christ up from death and Hades and caused Him to transcend far above the human beings on the earth and the evil angelic powers in the air and to sit at the peak of the universe. This power also subjected all things under His feet and gave Him to be the Head over all things to the church. Today we are enjoying the transmitting of the Lord's transcending power.